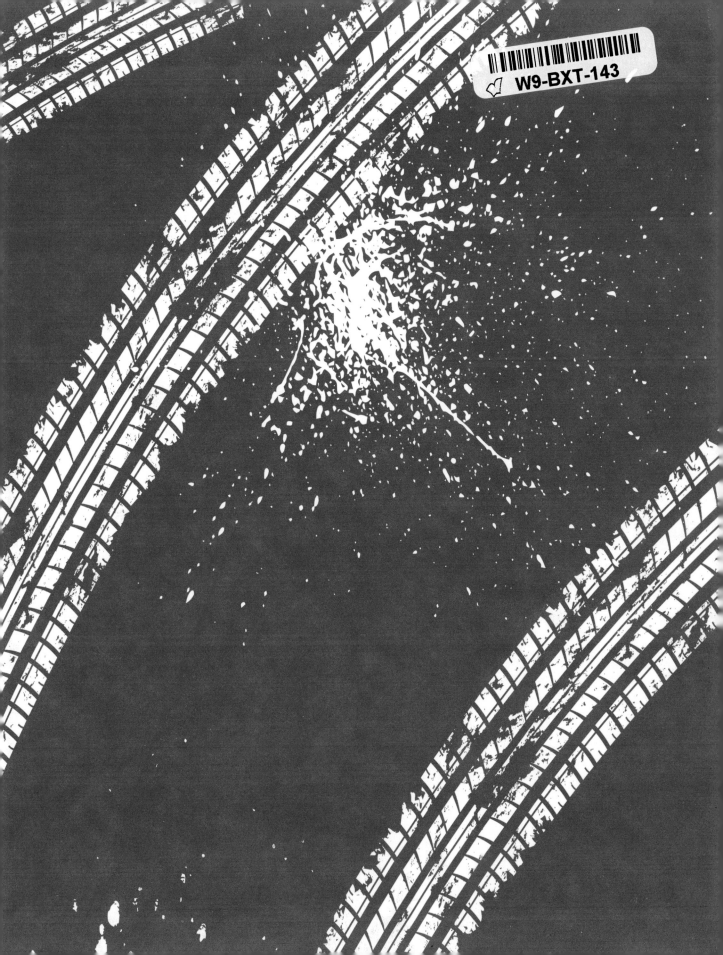

W9-BXT-143

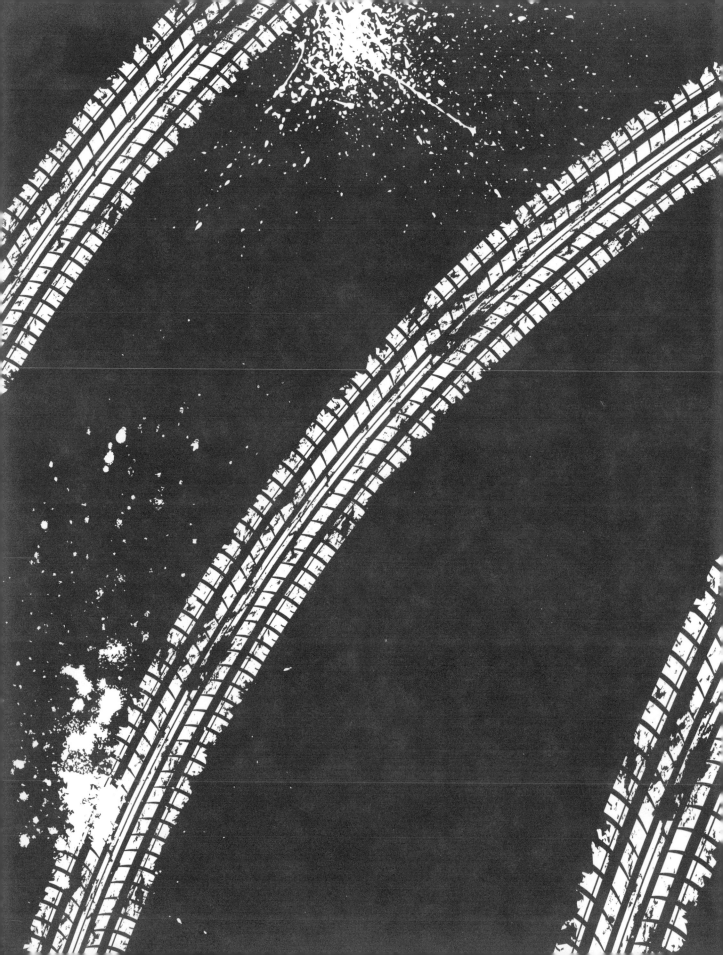

# ROAD & TRACK

# CR&W

# BIG & FAST CARS

# BIG&FAST CARS

## 701 TOTALLY AMAZING FACTS!

**Dan Bova**
and the editors of

# CONTENTS

"Racers, start your engines!
Readers, start your eyeballs!"

# START YOUR ENGINES!

Buckle up, you're holding the fastest page-turner on the planet!

This is the ultimate book for kids who love all kinds of cars, from slick supercars to powerful monster trucks to record-smashing racers. Inside you'll find amazing photos, mind-blowing facts, and answers to some very serious questions, like: *Do you know why the van was embarrassed around its friends? Because it had a little gas!*

For hundreds of years people have been imagining and building machines that go fast and look cool doing it (see pages 58-59). It's amazing how far innovations in car performance and design have come. Just think, many of the first cars were powered by steam engines, had no windshields, and drove on wheels made out of solid chocolate. (Okay, that last one is made up, but you believed us for a second, didn't you?) And now we have cars that drive themselves — for real! Speaking of which, ever wonder whose fault it is if two self-driving cars crash into each other? Turn to page 137 and find out.

As you flip through this book, you'll learn not just about automobiles, but about people who have amazing car-related careers designing, testing, and racing them, including a toymaker, an IndyCar superstar, a scientist who controls rovers on Mars, and someone who gets paid to find out exactly how fast Ferraris go. (We'd trade in our weekly chore of putting away the dishes in a heartbeat for that gig!) You'll also get a peek inside the garages of your favorite car-collecting celebs. Who knows, maybe one day you'll become best friends with The Rock and he'll loan you his $300,000 Rolls-Royce for your driver's test. (Probably not, but maybe!)

Anyway, there's so much more in this book, and the best way to find out what's in it is to turn the page and step on the gas.

## READY, SET, GO!

"So I can win this race and make s'mores at the same time? Sweet!"

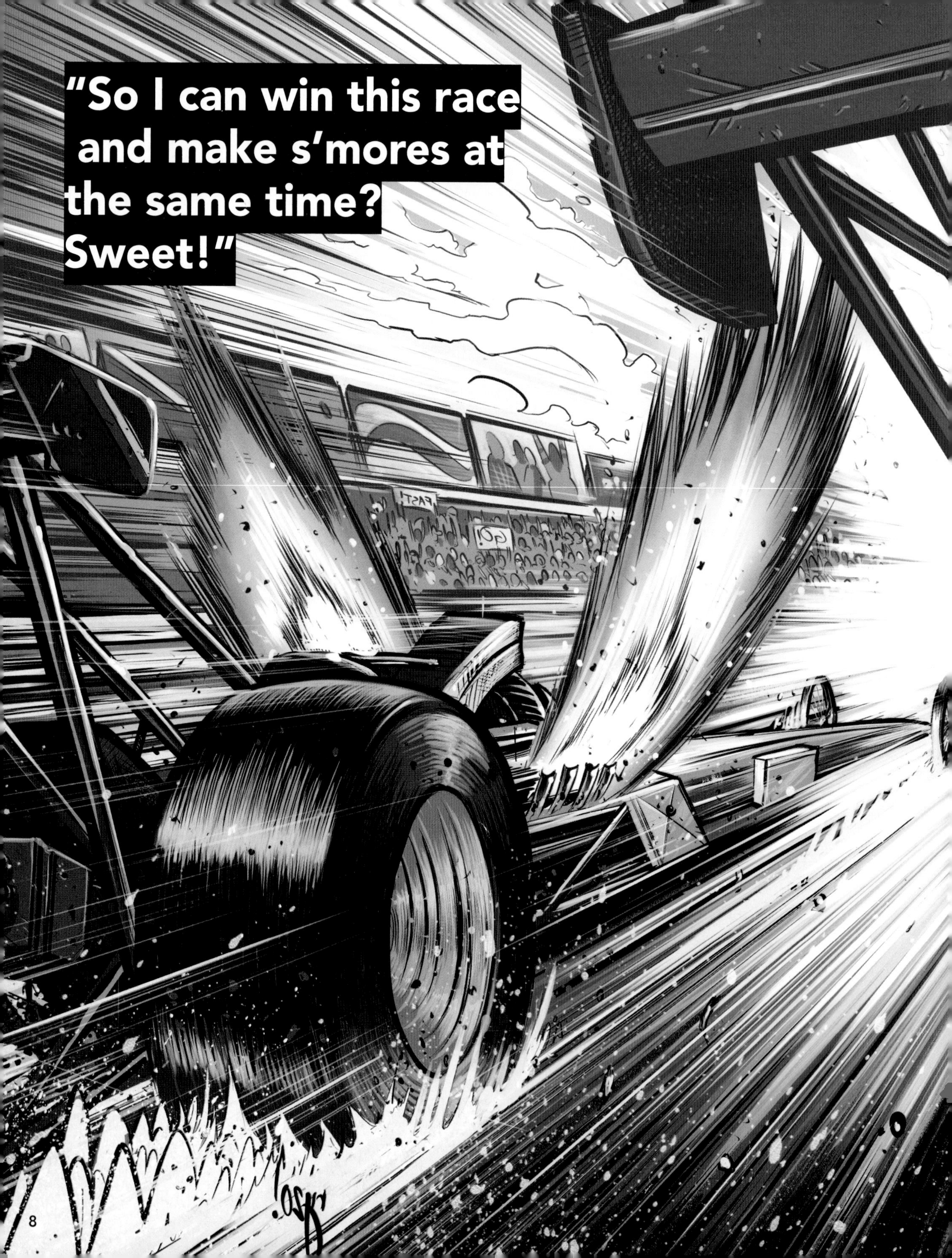

# CHAPTER 1

# SPEED ZONE

# HERE WE GO!

We have to hurry up with this introduction, because this is the **speed chapter** and everything in it is fast! So here are three quick questions for you:

Why did the car need a nap?
*Because it was tired.*

What has four wheels and flies?
*A garbage truck.*

Why are we hitting you with all of these groan-inducing jokes?
*To make you turn the page quicker and start reading.*

## DID IT WORK?

IT'S THE MOST POWERFUL LAMBO IN HISTORY!

# THE LAMBORGHINI ESSENZA SCV12'S V-12 ENGINE PRODUCES UPWARDS OF 819 HORSEPOWER.

## SOME TERMS YOU'LL SEE THROUGHOUT THIS CHAPTER:

| | |
|---|---|
| **CYLINDERS** | The part of the engine where gas and air ignite to produce power. |
| **HORSEPOWER (HP)** | Measure of power produced by a car's engine. |
| **HYBRID** | A car that is powered by both gasoline and electricity. |
| **MPH** | Miles per hour, how fast the car is going. |
| **RPM** | Revolutions per minute, a measure of how fast an engine's parts are moving. |
| **TACHOMETER** | A gauge on the dashboard that measures RPM. |
| **V-12** | V is the shape of how the cylinders are laid out in the engine, and 12 is the number of cylinders in the engine. If it were a V-8, that would mean it has eight cylinders. *(See page 22 for more details!)* |

# BUILT FOR SPEED

## SOME OF THE QUICKEST CARS EVER MADE!

The amount of time it takes a car to accelerate from 0 to 60 mph is a standard way to judge how awesome it performs. Here are some of the crazy-quickest rides on the road and their stop-watch-shattering times!

### 2019 LAMBORGHINI URUS

To put this SUV's acceleration into perspective, a Ford Explorer takes more than twice as long to hit 60 mph. Urus is a kind of bull, and this bull can run!

**3.1 SECONDS**

### 2019 FERRARI 488 PISTA

*Pista* is Italian for "track," which is where this beast was born to let loose.

**2.7 SECONDS**

### 2015 TESLA MODEL S P90D

Once upon a time, people thought electric cars had wimpy motors. Then this sedan hit the road and nearly blew off all four of its doors!

**2.7 SECONDS**

## 2019 BMW M5 COMPETITION

Don't be fooled by its normal looks. This four-door sedan is a jet fighter in disguise.

**2.6 SECONDS**

## 2019 MCLAREN 720S COUPE

How cool is this? The McLaren 720S has a launch button next to its radio, climate, and navigation controls. When the digital tachometer hits 3,200 rpm for four full seconds, "Boost Ready" flashes on the dashboard. Take off!

**2.6 SECONDS**

## 2018 LAMBORGHINI HURACÁN PERFORMANTE

Bring your earplugs! This monster V-10 engine roars at 100 decibels, which is about as loud as a giant freight train.

**2.3 SECONDS**

## 2015 PORSCHE 918 SPYDER

This hybrid speed demon is every bit as exotic looking as any near-million-dollar supercar should be. It has a reported top speed of 214 mph, and its cabin is more futuristic looking than the inside of Luke Skywalker's X-Wing!

**2.1 SECONDS**

# WHAT HAPPENS IF A RACE-CAR DRIVER HAS TO *PEE* DURING A RACE?

There aren't a lot of porta potties along the sides of racetracks. So what does a driver do if they really, really have to pee? A NASCAR fan asked racing legend Dale Earnhardt Jr. on Twitter how many times a year he went to the bathroom in his car and Earnhardt wasn't shy about sharing: "Once or twice a YEAR. When ya gotta go ya gotta go." Earnhardt told sports website For The Win that it is rare that a driver has to pee during a race, but when they do, it is better just to let it flow. Trying to hold it in can be quite a distraction, and you need total focus when driving a car over 200 mph. Sounds super gross, but Earnhardt does point out that it isn't that big a deal for drivers when you think about it: "You're hot and sweaty and soaking wet already!"

**DON'T TRY THIS AT HOME, KIDS!**

## HOW DOES THAT WORK?

# REAR SPOILER

You've seen that wing-like thing on the back of sports cars. No doubt they look supercool, but what exactly do they do? **Here's the surprising answer:** Even though they look like a wing designed to make a car take off, they do the exact opposite. When a car is driving, the air flowing around it creates lift, which loosens a car's grip on the road. A spoiler is like an upside-down wing — it is designed to push a car down, which increases its grip on the road. The only other way to make sure a superfast car doesn't fly off the track is to make it heavier. And when is the last time you heard about a 2-ton school bus winning the Indy 500?

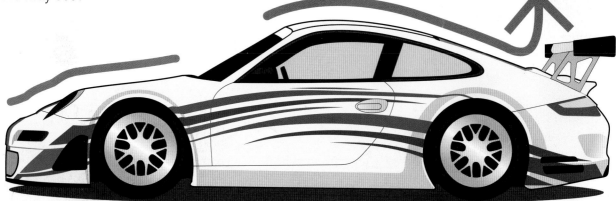

# A FAST-MOVING CAR

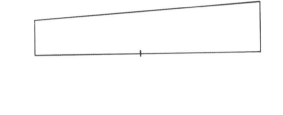

**1.** Let's start easy with a sloping rectangle. Use a pencil, because we're going to be doing a lot of erasing!

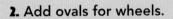

**2.** Add ovals for wheels.

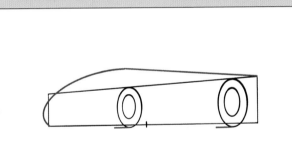

**3.** Give a rounded shape to the car's body and create depth for the wheels.

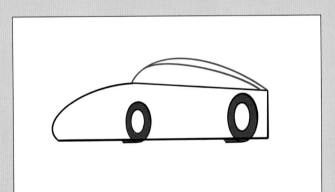

**4.** Color in the tires and add the roof.

**5.** Add shapes for lights, window partitions, and a front grille. Lastly...spoiler alert! Add a spoiler to give it a sporty look.

**6.** Time to floor it! Add burnout smoke from the tires and speed lines from the spoiler, roof, or wherever you want. There are no rules or speed limits where you're headed!

# COOL
## JOB ALERT!

# RACE CAR DRIVER

**ALEXANDER ROSSI IS AN ELITE RACER WHO WON THE INDY 500 DURING HIS ROOKIE SEASON! HE EXPLAINS WHAT IT'S LIKE TO BE A PROFESSIONAL SPEEDSTER.**

**What is something about being a race car driver that most people don't understand?**
You have to work out a lot! Going as fast as we do, there are G-forces that are like four to six times your body weight pressing against you. So you hold your breath, which raises your heart rate, which makes your body get fatigued. Plus, there is no power steering in our cars, so you need strength to control the wheel.

### Is it scary to drive over 200 mph?

Sometimes. Some of the oval tracks we drive on are really fast and you're side-by-side for a long time with the other cars. But when you've trained your whole life, you don't think about the scary parts of it so much — you think more about the potential that you have each weekend to win the race!

### Were you interested in racing as a kid?

Yes, it all started with my 10th birthday present. My dad took me to a go-kart school in Las Vegas and the coach was like, "He's actually pretty good. You should look into buying a go-kart." And my dad initially said no, but I kept pestering him about it. Finally, we bought a basic go-kart and did some club racing and it went well. That's how the journey started.

### IndyCar races are a couple of hours long. Do you get to listen to music during a race?

I wish we got listen to music! That would be really cool. But no, you just listen to a crew guy in your headset that is either happy or not happy about how things are going.

### Does your race car have a drink holder?

It kind of does, but not like a cup holder in a normal car. There is a CamelBak pack to the side of you that has a long tube. And there's a button on the steering wheel that you can press and it kind of squirts water, Gatorade, or whatever into your mouth.

### What was it like to win the Indy 500?

I think the coolest part about winning that race is your face goes on the trophy next to all the other winners. So my face is on the same trophy with drivers like Mario Andretti, Rick Mears, and A.J. Foyt. And that's pretty special that it will be there forever.

### The tradition is that the winner is handed a bottle of milk to drink at the end. How was that?

The bottled milk is a little bit weird, I'm going to be honest. It's cool that it's a tradition, but there's a lot of other drinks like water that would probably be my first choice after racing on a 95-degree day!

### How do you drive in regular life? Do you speed to the supermarket?

I used to, but then I got quite a few speeding tickets! I backed it down so I haven't gotten a ticket in like three or four years. So yeah, I pump the brakes a little bit more these days!

**"MY DAD BOUGHT A BASIC GO-KART AND WE DID SOME CLUB RACING AND IT WENT WELL. THAT'S HOW THE JOURNEY STARTED."**

# CAR-CRAZED CELEB
# DANICA PATRICK

The first woman to win an IndyCar Series race started racing go-karts when she was just 10 years old!

## DANICA'S MOST AMAZING MOMENTS

→ At the 2005 Indianapolis 500, she became the first woman to take the lead and score a top-five finish. Not bad for her first time!

→ In 2008, she made history as the first woman to win an IndyCar race.

→ Her third-place result in the 2009 Indy 500 made her the highest-finishing female driver in that race's history.

→ At the 2013 Daytona 500, she set the fastest qualifying time and became the first woman to nab the pole position. (The best spot at the start line.)

→ One of the reasons she chose number 10 for her Stewart Haas Racing Sprint Cup car is because that's how old she was when she started go-kart racing.

→ In 2015, she shattered the record for most top-10 finishes by any female in NASCAR.

→ She has appeared in 14 Super Bowl commercials!

→ Danica retired in 2018. That year, she became the first female host of ESPN's sports award show, the ESPYs.

> "WE ALL HAVE DREAMS. WE START OUT AS KIDS WHO WANT TO 'BE' OR 'DO' SOMETHING ONE DAY. THE TRICK IS TO FIND OUT WHAT BRINGS YOU JOY AND CREATE A LIFE FULL OF THAT. AND OF COURSE, TO DREAM BIG!"

# WHICH IS QUICKEST?

Pick the faster choice in these matchups.

**CORVETTE STINGRAY** VS. **TESLA ROADSTER**

**CYCLIST DENISE MUELLER-KORENEK** VS. **HONDA ACCORD**

**FERRARI 812 SUPERFAST** VS. **LAMBORGHINI VENENO**

**SCHOOL BUS** VS. **GARBAGE TRUCK**

**SNAIL** VS. **KETCHUP LEAVING A BOTTLE**

Check out the answers on page 140!

# HOW TO CALCULATE SPEED

**HERE'S AN EASY EXPERIMENT YOU CAN DO AT HOME TO FIND OUT HOW FAST SOMETHING IS MOVING.**

You'll need:

☐ Measuring tape
☐ A stopwatch
☐ A toy car, a ball, a cat — whatever!

**STEP 1** Measure out a 10-foot length on the floor, marking the start and end points with pieces of tape or books.

**STEP 2** Get the car or ball rolling from a few feet behind the start line.

**STEP 3** Start your stopwatch as soon as it hits the start line and stop it as soon as it crosses the finish line.

**STEP 4** Math time! Divide the distance (10 feet) by the amount of time it took the object to travel. For example, let's say it took two seconds.

**10 FEET ÷ 2 SECONDS = 5 FEET PER SECOND**

Wanna know the MPH? Grab a calculator (and an adult if you need).

To convert fps (feet per second) to mph (miles per hour), multiply the fps number by .68181818.

So 5 fps x .68181818 = 3.4 mph

**IF YOU TRAVELED 50 MILES IN 1/2 HOUR? YOU'D BE GOING 100 MPH. SLOW DOWN!**

# FILL IN THE BLANKS
# A RACE YOU'LL NEVER FORGET

Ask a friend for a word for each blank, but don't tell them what the story is about! Then read it back and get ready to laugh.

Welcome, racing fans, to the _____ 500!
<br>STREET YOU LIVE ON

We're in the final lap, and this has been a very _____ race. So far we
<br>ADJECTIVE

had a _____ car pileup, which officials believe happened because someone let
<br>HUGE NUMBER

_____ drive a car.
<br>NAME OF A PET

Driver _____ is now in third place, which is surprising,
<br>FAMILY MEMBER'S NAME

considering they cuddled with _____ and took a _____ -minute
<br>FAVORITE STUFFED ANIMAL NUMBER

nap during their last pit stop.

In second place is _____, who is grading your last _____
<br>NAME OF A TEACHER SCHOOL SUBJECT

test as they drive. It's hard to read their handwriting; you either got an A or a(n) _____
<br>ALPHABET LETTER

on it.

And in first place is _____ ! They have the windows rolled down and are
<br>ADULT FAMILY MEMBER'S NAME

blasting their favorite song, "_____ ."
<br>NAME OF A SONG YOU HATE

The crowd is cheering like crazy, except for _____ , who asked if the
<br>NAME OF A NEIGHBOR

drivers could please turn down the volume on their engines.

The cars are neck and neck, nose to nose, _____ to _____ .
<br>BODY PART ANOTHER BODY PART

They're in the final straightaway and the winner is … no one! They all got pulled over for

speeding by a(n) _____ traffic cop.
<br>ADJECTIVE

And so ends another _____ day at the races!
<br>ADJECTIVE

# MOMMY, WHERE DO VROOMS COME FROM?

We all know that you step on the gas and the car goes. But how exactly? Let's take a peek under the hood.

## HEART OF THE CAR

It's called an internal-combustion engine because it takes a bunch of gasoline, lights it on fire, and turns the resulting explosions into something called torque. Torque is a twisting force that's applied to the wheels, and off we go!

## PISTONS

These are components within the engine that move up and down inside metal tubes called cylinders. Depending on the vehicle, there are usually between four and 12 pistons and cylinders in an engine.

## KA-POW!

The pistons move up and down thanks to thousands of tiny explosions that are created when something called a spark plug ignites the fuel and oxygen mixture.

↑
**2021 CHEVROLET CORVETTE STINGRAY ENGINE**

## CYLINDERS

Each cylinder has an inlet valve, into which fuel and air are sprayed from a fuel injector.

## TURBOCHARGERS

While the Corvette engine in the photo doesn't use them, turbochargers and superchargers pump extra air into the engine, increasing the amount of oxygen and the amount of fuel that can be burned. Yep, all of those increases mean an increase in power and speed!

## CRANKSHAFT

The pistons connect to the car's crankshaft, which powers the car's gearbox, which turns the wheels.

## LITERS

6.2 LITERS

When pistons move, they suck in a certain amount of air, which varies depending on the size of the piston and how far it moves. Car manufacturers will tell you the total cubic liters of air a motor takes in because a higher number can equal more power produced. This one is 6.2 liters, which helps it generate 495 hp.

THE MORE CYLINDERS POWERING THE CRANKSHAFT, THE MORE POWER AND SPEED YOU GET.

WE'LL TAKE TWELVE, PLEASE!

# AROUND THE WORLD
# IN 8 RACES

**From sophisticated classics to flat-out nuttiness, here are the most famous races on wheels.**

# INDIANAPOLIS 500

**What is it:** A 500-mile IndyCar race, where drivers need to complete 200 laps around the legendary Indianapolis Motor Speedway, usually driving for more than three hours with only quick pit stops.

**Been there, drove that:** "I really need to be comfortable with the car and confident to challenge in that last stint. Laps 1-30 to Laps 170-200, it's such a different mentality. And I love it, I love the tension, I love the fact that after going 170 laps, this is your moment now. Be aggressive as you can and produce a great race. That's the feeling, and I've been there many years."
—Takuma Sato, 2017 and 2020 winner

*Fast fact: There is a tradition where the winner gets rewarded with a bottle of milk. Yum? See page 17 for Alexander Rossi's take on this tradition.*

# DAYTONA 500

**What is it:** A 500-mile NASCAR Cup Series race run at the Daytona International Speedway in Florida.

**Been there, drove that:** "I'm a student of the game. I never stop learning and trying to figure out where to put myself at the right time. It doesn't always work!...But I just trust my instincts and so far they've been good for me."
— Denny Hamlin, 2016, 2019, and 2020 winner

*Fast fact: Richard Petty holds the record for the most wins — 7! He won in 1964, 1966,1971,1973,1974, 1979, and 1981.*

# BAJA 1000

**What is it:** An incredibly brutal off-road race held on the Baja California Peninsula, Mexico.

**Been there, drove that:** "You get people from other states or other countries, and they really have no idea what they are getting into. Baja is much more desolate than people think. There's no signs telling you where to go so the more experience you have the better."
— Ivan "Ironman" Stewart, 1975, 1993, and 1998 winner

*Fast fact: There's one course but a lot of different race classes (groupings by vehicle type), from buggies to motorcycles to trucks.*

# THE PIKES PEAK INTERNATIONAL HILL CLIMB

**What is it:** Also known as The Race to the Clouds, it is a 12.42-mile race to the top of Pikes Peak, Colorado.

**Been there, drove that:** "It was a great achievement, because technology-wise the car [the all-electric Volkswagen I.D. R Pikes Peak] was so complicated and new that it took a big effort for the team."
— Romain Dumas, 2018 record-setting winner

*Fast fact: The race is held on a public toll road that has 156 turns and climbs 4,720 feet!*

Pikes Peak Highway
ELEVATION
13,000 Ft
3,962 m

# THE 24 HOURS OF LE MANS

**What is it:** A 24-hour race near the town of Le Mans, Fran that goes through a mix of public roads and a racetrack.

**Been there, drove that:** "There is never a stop, you rac in very different conditions, from the heat in the afterno through the night to the cold in the morning. And the track keeps changing!"
— Fernando Alonso, 2019 winning team member

*Fast fact: Each car has three drivers, who take two-hour shifts during the race. Power nap time!*

# MONACO GRAND PRIX

**What is it:** A Formula 1 race held on a narrow course that snakes its way through the streets of Monaco.

**Been there, drove that:** "[Winning feels] ridiculous, in all the right ways. It was a stressful race…But crossing the line felt amazing."
— Daniel Ricciardo, 2018 winner

*Fast fact: The 3.3-kilometer track has so many twists and turns that drivers must change gears 4,200 times*

# BATHURST 1000

**What is it:** A 1100-kilometer touring-car race held in New South Wales, Australia.

**Been there, drove that:** "It is unusual in some ways with blind corners and heavy compression in some places. It's a track I like because it's a rare place where it rewards bravery. There are not many tracks that do that anymore."
— Shane van Gisbergen (co-driver with Garth Tander), 2020 winner

*Fast fact:* The endurance race is usually run with a pair of drivers for each car, but there have been a number of drivers who went on their own. (They all lost.)

# DAKAR RALLY

**What is it:** A grueling off-road race that has changed locations over the years. Most recently it was a 4,900-mile race through Saudi Arabia.

**Been there, drove that:** "It's a race you need to respect and prepare a lot for, especially if you're a veteran like me. I love competition, I love winning, and this is a great challenge, where you push your body and your brain to the limit. The fact that you're competing for 12 days on stages longer than 500 km makes it a special event for everybody."
— Carlos Sainz, 2010, 2018, and 2020 winner

*Fast fact:* One year, a competitor was struck by lightning during the race — and he finished anyway!

# THE
# RECORD-BREAKING

## TEEN SPEED MACHINE
## CHLOE CHAMBERS

When Chloe Chambers broke a driving record at the age of 16, she had already had a lot of practice. The driving superstar first got behind the wheel of a vehicle when she was just seven years old!

Chloe took her first driving lesson in 2011, and a year later, became Kid Kart Champion at Oakland Valley Race Park. Talk about a fast learner! Many wins and trophies quickly followed, including securing a spot in the Guinness Book of World Records for the fastest vehicle slalom in 2020.

To break the record, Chambers had to zip through 50 cones spaced 15.05 meters apart in less than 48.11 seconds. Behind the wheel of a 2020 Porsche 718 Spyder, she did it in 47.45 seconds.

It's quite an accomplishment, but Chloe says she's not done wowing driving fans. "I strive to be the best that I can be as a person. In motorsports, my goal is to not just compete in Formula 1, but to be competitive there."

Chloe says she loves everything about racing, especially the competitive part. "I like how so many factors play a role in your performance. The complexity makes victories feel so much better, because there's so much of a team effort that goes into each one," she explains.

Any other records she has her eye on? "Not necessarily Guinness World Records,". says Chloe, "but I am definitely looking to break more track records."

# CLUB

Meet the people, animals, and machines that the Guiness Book of World Records has declared the fastest in their field.

### FASTEST CAR

The Thrust SSC doesn't just look like a rocket, it acts like one. In 1997, driver Andy Green took it out for a cruise that set a land-speed record of 763.035 mph. That's 2 mph faster than the speed of sound!

### FASTEST MAMMAL

Cheetahs can run 60-70 mph. (Note: Do not try to play tag with a cheetah.) After chasing prey like hares and impalas, they sometimes need half an hour to catch their breath before they dig in.

### FASTEST HUMAN-POWERED BIKE

Engineers and students at the University of Toronto built the Team Aerovelo Eta bike which won the World Human Powered Speed Challenge at a leg-numbing 86.65 mph!

## SPEEDY

### FASTEST HUMAN

On August 16, 2009, lightning-fast sprinter Usain Bolt won the World Championships 100-meter run in 9.58 seconds. He hit a peak speed of 27.34 mph, and, no, his sneakers didn't have mini engines hidden inside of them!

### FASTEST MOBILITY SCOOTER

Inventor Colin Furze built a mobility scooter in his garage that can go 82.5 mph. (Most go around 4 mph.) His high-speed secret? A Honda motorbike engine under the seat!

### FASTEST MOTORCYCLE

With a top speed of 420 mph, the Dodge Tomahawk is the fastest — and probably coolest-looking — motorcycle ever made. It accelerates from 0 to 60 mph in 2.5 seconds, so careful with the throttle!

## FAST FACTS!

### HERE ARE SOME INTERESTING FACTS TO GET YOU THINKING!

The most expensive speeding ticket was given to a driver in Switzerland who was going 85 mph in a 50-mph zone. The fine? **$290,000!**

The "500" in race names like the Indy 500 and Daytona 500 signifies the race's length: **500 miles.**

# 500

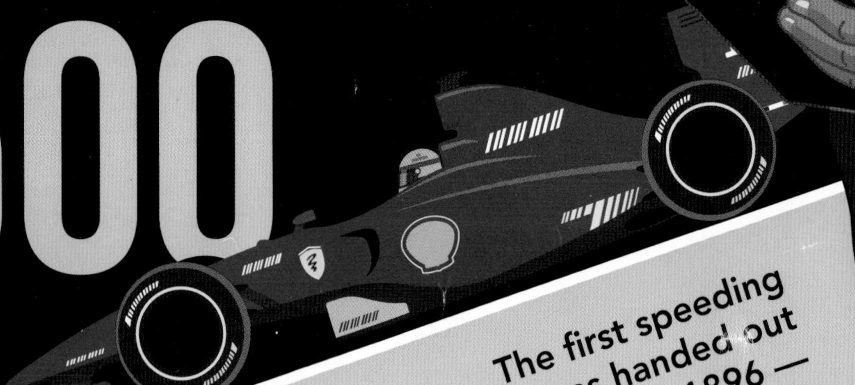

The first speeding ticket was handed out to a driver in 1896 — for going 8 mph in a 2-mph zone!

KEEP ← LEFT

KEEP → RIGHT

## 35% VS. 65%

Thirty-five percent of the world's people drive on the left side of the road. Sixty-five drive on the right. **Who's right?**

IndyCar race teams spend around $225,000 on tires during a season!

The city of Dubai has the fastest police cruiser in the world — a Bugatti Veyron that can hit a top speed of 253 mph!

**95%**

The average car spends 95 percent of its lifetime parked. And we thought we were lazy!

There are an estimated 1.2 billion cars on the road around the world. No wonder finding a parking spot is so hard!

## SPEED MAP MINDBUSTER

Let's test your memory: Can you put these things that were mentioned in this chapter in order of slowest to speediest?

☐ 2015 Porsche 918 Spyder

☐ Ketchup leaving a bottle

☐ Thrust SSC

☐ Mobility scooter

☐ Usain Bolt

☐ Bugatti Veyron

Check out the answers on page 140!

The wheel was invented around 3500 BCE. Those caveman carpools must have been a hoot.

"I knew I shouldn't have gotten out of bed this morning," thought the red car.

# CHAPTER 2

# RUGGED RIDES
## POWER UP!

# VROOM!

Hey, what did you say? Sorry, we can't hear you. This is the power chapter, and it sometimes gets pretty loud!

On the following pages, you will learn about record-smashing drivers, the world's most powerful vehicles, and the precise thought that goes through a person's head as they fly 30 feet through the air inside a 12,000-pound truck. *(Hint: It rhymes with* **"AAAAAAHHHHHH!"**)

**WHEN IT COMES TO DRIVING OVER ROCKS, THIS MONSTER, WELL, ROCKS!**

## SOME TERMS YOU'LL SEE THROUGHOUT THIS CHAPTER:

| | |
|---|---|
| **BRAKE HORSEPOWER (BHP)** | It's like horsepower (see page 11), but it takes into account the power that is lost due to friction in the engine parts. One bhp is slightly less than 1 hp. |
| **DIESEL** | A type of fuel and type of engine that produces a lot of torque. (See below for what this means!) |
| **4X4** | Four-wheel drive, which means the engine delivers torque to all of its wheels at the same time. |
| **RANGE** | How far a vehicle can travel on a single tank of fuel or battery charge. |
| **SEMI TRUCK** | You know when you see big tractor trailer? The semi is the truck half (where the engine and driver are). |
| **TON** | A unit of measure for weight that is equal to 2,000 pounds. |
| **TORQUE** | The twisting force, or strength, of an engine that gets a vehicle moving. (Note: Torque rhymes with pork!) |

## THE TROPHY TRUCK IN THIS PICTURE IS DRIVEN BY SUPERSTAR OFF-ROADER BJ BALDWIN, AND IT HAS 800 BHP UNDER THE HOOD!

# VEHICLES ON EARTH

Our advice if you see one of these beasts coming down the road? Get out of the way!

## ← SHOCKWAVE JET TRUCK

This crazy truck is equipped with three huge jet engines, giving it a combined 36,000 hp! Not only is it the mightiest truck in the known universe, it also holds the semi-truck speed record of 376 mph.

## → 2022 GMC HUMMER

Maybe you want something that will actually fit in your driveway? Well, here you go. This four-door electric pickup truck has a 350-mile range and is powered by an eco-friendly engine that produces 1,000 hp. Who knew that saving the planet could be so fun?

### → NASA CRAWLER-TRANSPORTER

When NASA needs to move its launch pads, rockets, and spacecrafts, they call in one of their two crawler-transporters, which can carry over 6 million pounds...very slowly. Don't climb in one for a quick ride to the astronaut snack bar; crawler-transporters have a top speed of 2 mph.

### ↑ LETOURNEAU L-2350

The biggest earth mover on planet Earth can scoop up 80 tons, has 13-foot-tall tires, and is equipped with a 16-cylinder diesel engine that puts out 2,300 hp. One of its engineers told the History Channel, "We can dig an Olympic-size swimming pool in just a few scoops." Cannonball!

**SEE MORE AWESOME SPEED MACHINES ON PAGE 66!**

# BACK TO SCHOOL Blast!

Being late for school will never be a problem if you're getting a lift in this totally bonkers bus! Gerd Habermann Racing Group first showed off its Jet Bus at the Essen Motor Show in Germany. The yellow speed machine rockets forward thanks to a 25,000 horsepower Westinghouse J34 turbojet engine that was used in many military fighter planes. Yes, it is extremely powerful, but on your way to school, you're going to need to make a lot of stops for fuel. It only gets an estimated 0.015 miles per gallon!

## SCHOOLS WITH NO BRAKES!

If you have a need for speed, here are some of the top go-karting tracks in the world that'll get you on the fast track to racing glory.

**Sugar River Raceway in Brodhead, WI.** This is where superstar NASCAR and Indy driver Danica Patrick got her start!

**Dubai Autodrome in Dubai, UAE.** It features an indoor track and an outdoor circuit that with 17 corners, a tunnel, and a bridge to keep things interesting.

**CalSpeed Karting Center in Los Angeles, CA.** Located at the Auto Club Speedway), the CalSpeed race track has a ¾-mile circuit that can be configured to have up to 15 turns.

**South Garda Karting in Brescia, Italy.** If you're ever in Italy, go see a sculpture by Michelangelo, try some pizza, and take a turn on this legendary karting track where many F1 greats have revved their engines.

# COOL JOB ALERT!

# CAR TESTER

**K.C. COLWELL IS THE DEPUTY TESTING DIRECTOR OF *CAR AND DRIVER* MAGAZINE. IT'S HIS JOB TO MEASURE CARS' ACCELERATION, TOP SPEED, BRAKING POWER, AND MORE. WHAT IS IT LIKE TO HAVE A JOB DRIVING AWESOME NEW CARS AROUND ALL DAY LONG? LET'S FIND OUT!**

**So wait, your job is to hit the gas and find out how fast cars can go? Is that as fun as it sounds?**

That is one part of it, and it is for sure a fun part. We drive cars as fast as they can possibly go, so safety is my number-one concern at the track. We're out there to make sure our facts are correct about the vehicles we write about, but that isn't as fun as driving fast.

**2019 MCLAREN SENNA: ZERO TO 60 MPH IN 2.8 SECONDS**

**How many cars do you think you've driven?**
In 16 years, I've driven more than 3000 cars.

**Do you have any favorites?**
I have been lucky to drive some very rare cars, including some race cars, but the Porsche 918 Spyder that I drove over three days at Virginia International Raceway remains the most special. And a Rolls-Royce is always special. The quality and craftsmanship is pretty incredible. Plus, a "Roller" is just super-quiet. It's like driving a cloud.

**What's the fastest you've driven?**
Just over 200 mph in a Bugatti Veyron, but reaching 184 mph in a not-so-aerodynamic 2009 Bentley Brooklands is a highlight.

**What's something about cars like Ferraris and Lamborghinis that is surprising the first time you get in one?**
I was surprised at how easy they are to drive and get comfortable in. The sounds, too. Nothing sounds the same as an Italian engine.

**Do they ever let you keep any of the supercars you test?**
I wish! I certainly try to keep them as long as possible. And I maybe once "misplaced" the keys, but in the end, they all go back.

**What were your favorite subjects in school?**
Math and science were always my favorite subjects. I liked that the answers are either right or wrong, and there was no interpretation. For my job, we apply a scientific method to testing cars. We know exactly how quick, fast, and grippy cars are. There is no way to misinterpret our data.

**Any other cool things about your very cool job?**
When I started testing cars it became evident that I was also pretty quick on a racetrack, and I now hold an unofficial track record. No one has lapped Virginia International Raceway's Grand Course in any car faster than I have in a 2019 McLaren Senna. That's pretty cool to me. The days when it is just me, a car, and a racetrack are the best days.

**K.C.'S MOST MEMORABLE RIDES**

BUGATTI VEYRON: COSTS OVER $2 MILLION.

PORSCHE 918 SPYDER: 211-MPH TOP SPEED.

ROLLS-ROYCE: ICONIC HOOD ORNAMENT CALLED THE SPIRIT OF ECSTASY.

2009 BENTLEY BROOKLANDS: ONLY 550 MADE!

# WHY DO THEY CALL IT "HORSEPOWER"?

In 1776 a mechanical wiz named James Watt designed a new, more efficient steam engine. In the hopes of selling his design to farmers and miners, who used animals to move lots of heavy stuff, he came up with a unit of measure that showed how many hoofed helpers his engine could replace: horsepower (hp). Watt studied animals at work and, with his business partner, determined that one horse had the power to lift 33,000 pounds one foot in one minute. Today, most engineers break it down as 1 hp equals 550 lb-ft per second. Impressive! And also convenient. Can you imagine getting driven to school by 200 horses instead of a 200-hp SUV? That could get pretty messy!

## HOW DOES THAT WORK? TURBOCHARGER

Engines require fuel and air to run. So to make more power, they need more air and more fuel! A turbocharger is a device that forces additional air into an engine to do just that. The turbocharger consists of two rotating propellers (a turbine and a compressor) that are connected together by a shaft. The flow of burnt gasses exiting the engine gets these two fan-like parts spinning (at speeds as high as 200,000 rpm), which forces additional air into the engine to produce the most teeth-rattling, head-snapping power possible!

# ? DID YOU KNOW?

## CORVETTES ONCE HAD A DIFFERENT NAME

When you hear the name Corvette, you think a car with a lot of speed and power. Now what do you think of when you hear the name "Project Opel"? That was the original moniker of this iconic car, and just like you, the people running Chevrolet thought it stunk. An executive named Myron Scott started looking for words in the dictionary that started with "C" (because it would sound nice with "Chevy") and stopped on the word "corvette." A corvette, he read, is a kind of fast ship used to escort military destroyers and gunboats. It sounded cool to everyone, and that's how one of the most famous cars in history got its name!

THE 2020 CHEVROLET CORVETTE C8 GOES [...] IN UNDER THREE SECONDS THANKS TO ITS 495-HP V-8 ENGINE (SEE PAGE 22 TO HAVE A LOOK AT ITS ENGINE).

# OFF-ROAD

## NO ROAD? NO PROBLEM FOR THESE DIRT-LOVING RIDES!

### MASERATI MC20

Maserati's 621-hp beast performs so well on regular roads and tracks, the designers decided to test it out in snowy and ice-covered conditions. No shocker, it drove like a dream. Bring on the snow days!

### LAMBORGHINI HURACÁN STERRATO

This experimental supercar is designed for "challenging environments." Thank goodness, we get so bored driving our Lambos around on flat, smooth streets.

### CUSTOM OFF-ROAD 964-GENERATION PORSCHE 911

It's powered by a 365-hp engine, but that's not the only big number attached to this custom-built off-roader. Its super-fancy version costs $650,000!

## FORD BRONCO R

In 1969, the Bronco was the first production 4x4 to win the Baja 1000. This new model was designed to grab that trophy again.

## ELECTRIC ODYSSEY 21 OFF-ROAD RACER

This rally beast's 550-hp motor allows it to go more than 60 mph while climbing a 56-degree incline. That's not straight up, but it is pretty darn close!

## SHERP ALL-TERRAIN AMPHIBIOUS VEHICLE

This ATV can drive over just about anything, and if a river gets in your way? It can float right across it. (That's great and all, but can it make us pancakes?)

# THE CRAZIEST ROADS IN THE WORLD!

**YOU'LL NEED A TOUGH CAR — AND MAYBE A PARACHUTE — TO CRUISE THESE UNTAMED HIGHWAYS SAFELY.**

## TIANMEN MOUNTAIN ROAD
**Where: China**

There are 99 twists and turns on this roadway as it snakes seven miles up to a top height of 4,265 feet.

## ATLANTIC ROAD
**Where: Norway**

This twisty coastal road has tons of crazy turns, and the weather conditions change so fast that you might suddenly not be able to see anything — including the huge waves that can crest over the road's barriers.

## DALTON HIGHWAY
**Where: Fairbanks, Alaska**

There are only three towns along this 413 miles of freezing-cold highway. Need help changing a flat tire? Ask a moose.

## NORTH YUNGAS ROAD
**Where: Bolivia**

Are you serious? This super-skinny dirt road travels up through the jungle to a height of 15,256 feet with steep drops on the sides!

# WHY DO PEOPLE GET CARSICK?

Motion sickness (you know, barfing in a car, plane, or boat) is not fun. Even thinking about it can make you nauseous. (Imagine how we feel researching and writing about it!) **Here's the scoop on what makes you want to spew:** It's caused by too many mixed-up signals hitting your brain at once, and your brain is like, "I can't deal with this right now." As explained by *BBC Earth Lab*, if you are looking down reading a book in the back of a car or bus, your eyes are telling you that you are stationary. But at the same time, all of the noises around you tell your ears that you are bopping around and zooming forward. This confusion of senses causes confusion in your noggin, which is why you end up feeling dizzy and sometimes get to see what you had for lunch all over again. Ugh, we're going to go lie down now.

## HOW DOES THAT WORK?

Want to have the most fun math and science lesson ever? Jump into a bumper car! The thing that makes crashing into your friends so fun is called physics. Specifically, **Newton's Laws of Motion.** The laws were written by Sir Isaac Newton, that super-smart guy who supposedly discovered the law of gravity after an apple fell on his head.

Newton figured out that every action creates an equal and opposite reaction. So if you bash your bumper car full force into another car, that car is going to go flying with the same force in the other direction! That would be pretty painful, if it weren't for the bumper cars' bumpers. Those rubber linings soften the smashup, and since they are mushy they change the angle of impact, which sends the cars spinning in unexpected directions. Buckle up, physics is rough stuff!

# BUMPER CARS

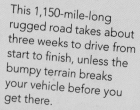

### GUOLIANG TUNNEL ROAD
**Where: China**
The inside of this 3/4-mile-long road tunnel is just 15 feet tall and 12 feet wide, making it really hard not to crash into its walls. Pillars carved into the rock are the only thing helping vehicles not fall off the edge!

### PASO DE LOS LIBERTADORES
**Where: Chile/Argentina**
Located in the Andes Mountains, this road runs up to 10,500 feet high!

### STELVIO PASS
**Where: Italy**
At an elevation of 9,045 feet above sea level, this is the highest paved mountain pass in the Eastern Alps. It has nearly 100 hairpin turns, and some say it looks like "a giant strand of spaghetti dropped from the heavens."

### CANNING STOCK ROUTE
**Where: Australia**
This 1,150-mile-long rugged road takes about three weeks to drive from start to finish, unless the bumpy terrain breaks your vehicle before you get there.

# WHAT'S IT LIKE TO DRIVE A MONSTER TRUCK?

**Krysten Anderson** is the first female driver of the most famous monster truck ever, Grave Digger! She earned the Guinness World Record title for highest ramp jump in a monster truck, flying 33.8 feet in the air! We asked her what driving a truck is like (after she landed, of course).

**How long have you been driving Monster Jam trucks?**
I've been driving Monster Jam trucks for four years.

**How big are they? Ever go through a drive-thru in one?**
Monster Jam trucks are, on average, 12 feet tall, 12 feet wide and weigh over 12,000 pounds. Your average drive-thru is about 6.5 to 7 feet tall — Grave Digger is almost twice that size! Maybe they would give me free chicken nugs if I did try to go through one?

**What was it like the first time you got behind the wheel?**
I was so nervous and so excited. I would compare driving Monster Jam trucks to riding the biggest, fastest roller coaster at the amusement park. Except you're driving and that roller coaster is also attached to a rocket!

**What stunt are you proudest of?**
The Guinness World Record title for the highest ramp jump in a monster truck!

**What is going through your head as you're soaring through the air?**
AHHHHHHHHHHH!!!

**How do you prepare for something like that?**
I would say it's more mental preparation than anything. Trying to convince yourself that you're capable of something that spectacular can be a challenge in itself. I think having my family and friends there to support me was a big key to my success. Also, I'm not one that accepts failures very well, so the thought of failing the stunt pushed me to go faster and push the truck harder! I wasn't going to give up.

**How do you invent new tricks?**
Most new tricks that we invent are actually happy accidents. A silly mistake we do during a run might actually turn out to be pretty entertaining to watch. Now figuring out how to do that "mistake" again is the tricky part!

**Your dad created Grave Digger and your brothers are drivers, too. Who is the biggest daredevil in your family?**
Hmm, that's a tough one to answer. My brothers and I are all equally crazy, but my brother Ryan pushes the envelope for certifiably insane.

**Does it feel weird when you drive normal-size cars?**
Yes and no. I think driving a Monster Jam truck has actually aided me in becoming a better daily driver. I feel like I have better control of my vehicle because I'm usually controlling one that's three times its size! If I can park Grave Digger in a tight spot, I can park any car.

**Do you listen to the radio when you're driving a monster truck? Do they have cup holders?**
I actually do have a cup holder in my truck for bottles of water I drink between events. As for the music, I think my engine would be louder than my radio, but I can actually hear my crew guy talking to me in my communication radio that is in my helmet. I can even talk back to my crew guy by pressing a button on my switch panel. It's just like using a walkie-talkie.

**You're the first female driver of Grave Digger. What words of advice do you have for kids who one day want to achieve an awesome accomplishment?**
Grave Digger has been in my family for three generations now. It had only been driven by men for 35 years. In January of 2017, I made history by being the first and only woman to pilot the legendary truck. This was very big news for Monster Jam back then. I have since had countless victories, made a little history, and even set world records in my short career. It's my goal to be an example for the younger generations (or even the older ones) that it doesn't matter what you look like or who you are — do not ever accept "no" for an answer. If you want it, go get it. It's yours. Prove to everyone (and yourself) that you can, and you will do it if you never give up. Whether it's big history or little history, go make it!

CRUSHIN' IT

# WHICH TiRE GOES WHERE?

## Do you know which terrain these tires are designed for?

**A.**

**B.**

**C.**

**D.**

**E.**

**F.**

**1.**

**2.**

**3.**

**4.**

**5.**

**6.**

Check out the answers on page 140!

# CAR-CRAZED CELEB
# THE ROCK!

Dwayne "The Rock" Johnson is insanely funny, talented and inspiring. But the superstar recently admitted to Jimmy Kimmel that everything in his life isn't perfect. "I have this problem," he admitted. "It's like a little sickness that I have: I really enjoy buying cars and giving cars to people."

The Rock went on to explain that one of his favorite hobbies is giving cool cars to his friends, family members and people who work for him. But if you do happen to become best buds with The Rock, remember this secret for snatching a sweet ride: "I give them to people I know — but if they ask, then I don't give it to them!"

## THE ROCK'S WILD RIDES
The superstar sure knows how to turn heads at his movie premieres!

← Commuting with Kevin Hart to *Jumanji:The Next Level.*

↑ Coming in hot to *San Andreas.*

↑ *Fast & Furious* (Well, actually kind of happy.)

# WHICH MEAN MACHINE IS RIGHT FOR YOU?

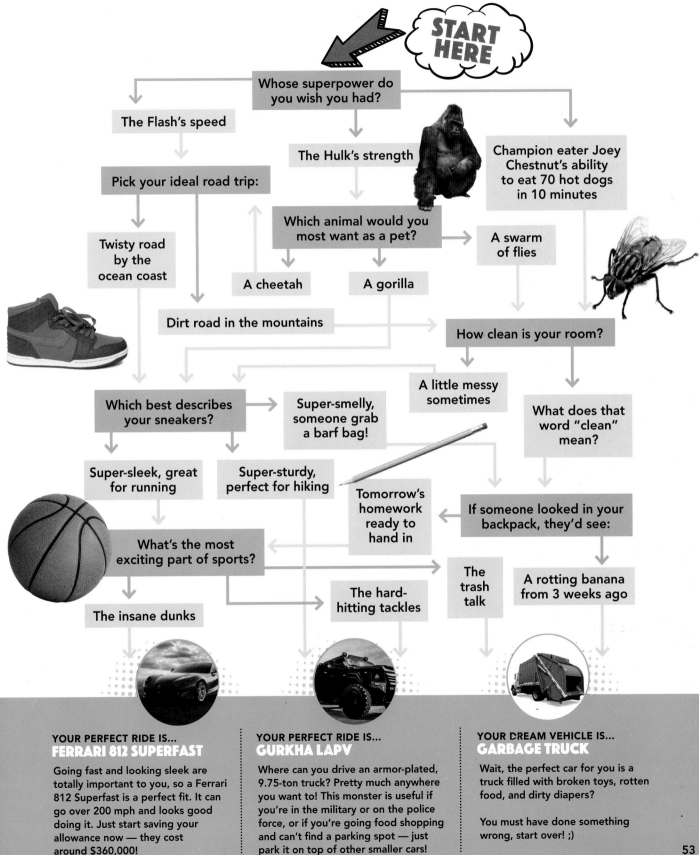

**START HERE**

Whose superpower do you wish you had?

- The Flash's speed
- The Hulk's strength
- Champion eater Joey Chestnut's ability to eat 70 hot dogs in 10 minutes

Pick your ideal road trip:

- Twisty road by the ocean coast
- Dirt road in the mountains

Which animal would you most want as a pet?

- A cheetah
- A gorilla
- A swarm of flies

How clean is your room?

- A little messy sometimes
- What does that word "clean" mean?

Which best describes your sneakers?

- Super-sleek, great for running
- Super-sturdy, perfect for hiking

Super-smelly, someone grab a barf bag!

If someone looked in your backpack, they'd see:

- Tomorrow's homework ready to hand in
- The trash talk
- A rotting banana from 3 weeks ago

What's the most exciting part of sports?

- The insane dunks
- The hard-hitting tackles

## YOUR PERFECT RIDE IS...
### FERRARI 812 SUPERFAST

Going fast and looking sleek are totally important to you, so a Ferrari 812 Superfast is a perfect fit. It can go over 200 mph and looks good doing it. Just start saving your allowance now — they cost around $360,000!

## YOUR PERFECT RIDE IS...
### GURKHA LAPV

Where can you drive an armor-plated, 9.75-ton truck? Pretty much anywhere you want to! This monster is useful if you're in the military or on the police force, or if you're going food shopping and can't find a parking spot — just park it on top of other smaller cars!

## YOUR DREAM VEHICLE IS...
### GARBAGE TRUCK

Wait, the perfect car for you is a truck filled with broken toys, rotten food, and dirty diapers?

You must have done something wrong, start over! ;)

53

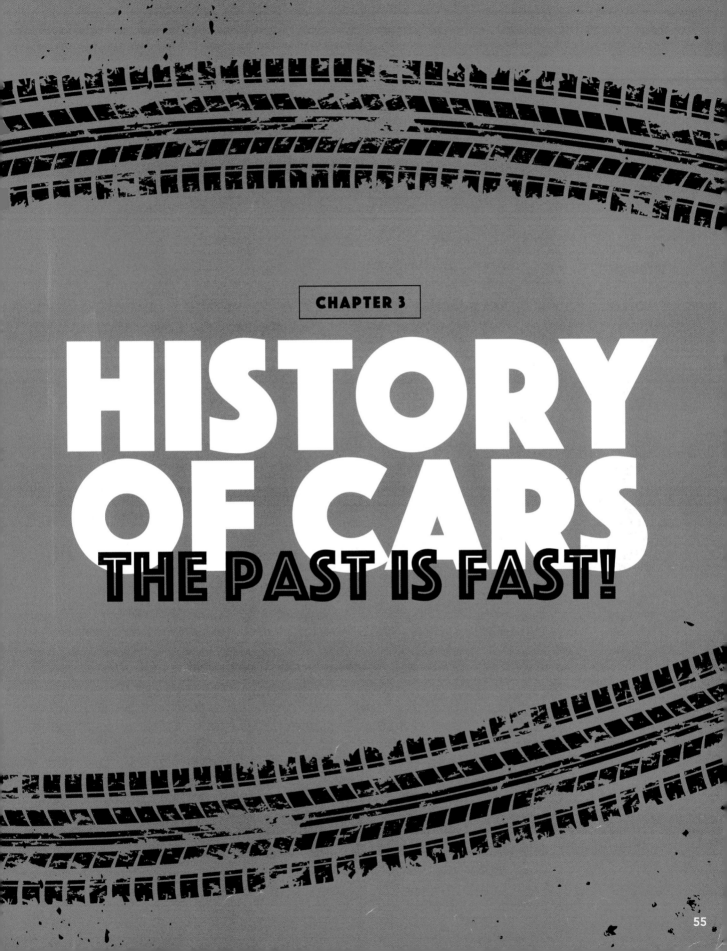

# CHAPTER 3

# HISTORY OF CARS
## THE PAST IS FAST!

# LET THE GOOD TIMES ROLL

When it comes to the history of automobiles, time goes by fast!

And to get us all in the mood to study the past, here's a really old joke:

What do you get when dinosaurs crash their cars? *Tyrannosaurus wrecks.*

IN 2011, RM SOTHEBY'S AUCTIONED THIS OFF FOR $4.6 MILLION!

THIS CAR, CALLED LA MARQUISE, WAS BUILT IN FRANCE IN 1884 AND IS BELIEVED TO BE THE OLDEST CAR IN THE WORLD THAT STILL RUNS. ITS STEAM-POWERED ENGINE (FUELED BY BURNING COAL, WOOD, AND PAPER) CAN GET THIS BABY GOING UP TO 38 MPH.

*La Marquise*

## SOME TERMS YOU'LL SEE THROUGHOUT THIS CHAPTER:

| | |
|---|---|
| **ASSEMBLY LINE** | A process for building a car where parts are added by workers as the car moves from station to station. This makes the process go way faster. |
| **GPS** | Global Positioning System, a navigation system that uses at least 24 satellites orbiting Earth to pinpoint where you are. |
| **GT** | "Gran Turismo" or "Grand Touring." It's a term Italian carmakers came up with to describe vehicles designed to transport people in speed and comfort. |
| **SLAMMED** | Modifying a car's body so that it sits lower to the ground and looks super-cool. |

# MOST AMAZING

## GET READY FOR THE FASTEST HISTORY LESSON YET!

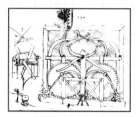

### 1478
Famous artist and inventor Leonardo da Vinci makes the first known sketch of a self-propelled car. He's the same guy who created the *Mona Lisa*, so his car probably had an *amazing* paint job!

### 1823
English engineer and inventor Samuel Brown invents the internal combustion engine, a technology that is still used today.

### 1863
Belgian engineer Jean-Joseph-Étienne Lenoir invents the "horseless carriage," the first commercially successful vehicle to use an internal combustion engine. "What are we supposed to do now?" asked the horses.

### 1908
Henry Ford's Model T first revs its engine, and, with help from the assembly line, about 15 million are eventually made. Imagine trying to find yours in a parking lot!

### 1914
Dodge introduces the first vehicle made with a steel body instead of wood. Would you trust a wooden car?

### 1769
Nicolas-Joseph Cugnot builds the first self-propelled road vehicle. It has three wheels and goes about 2.5 mph. Speed up, buddy!

### 1845
Robert William Thomson develops a more comfortable tire that is a rubber donut filled with compressed air. While they give a much smoother ride than solid-rubber tires, they're not nearly as delicious as regular donuts.

### 1884
Shocking news: This is the year that the first production electric car hits the road.

### 1911
Charles Kettering and Henry M. Leland develop the electric starter for engines to replace the hand crank. Sore arms everywhere say thank you.

### 1924
The car radio is introduced, and family road trips instantly get 97 percent less boring.

# INNOVATIONS

**1938**
The blinker becomes the standard way to tell someone behind you, "I'm pulling into this Taco Bell."

**1951**
John W. Hetrick registers his patent for the airbag. Almost every car on the road has an airbag these days. Guess you could say his invention really blew up!

**1968**
Seatbelts become required for all cars. Thousands of lives are saved every year thanks to seatbelts, so buckle up!

**1996**
General Motors begins a world of connected cars with its OnStar system, which uses your phone to call 911 in case of an accident. It does not, however, call Domino's in case of a snack attack.

**2014**
Elon Musk's company, Tesla, is the first to offer autopilot. Their Model S can steer and change lanes itself. But sadly for your parents, it doesn't allow the driver to nap on the way to 8 a.m. soccer games.

**1940**
Thank goodness air conditioning is introduced to cars. No more sweat — sweet!

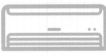

**1956**
A 1956 Buick Centurion concept car has the first rear camera. Instead of a rearview mirror, a television camera pointed out of the back and sent images to a screen in the dashboard. Smile!

**1995**
Cars get GPS (Global Positioning System). The era of trying to fold up giant roadmaps is finally over!

**1997**
Toyota Prius becomes the first mass-market hybrid car in the world. Hybrid cars use gas and electric power, making driving fun and eco-friendly.

**2020**
At the Consumer Electronics Show (CES), Hyundai shows off its Sonata Hybrid that has a solar-paneled roof they say will increase the vehicle's annual range by about 800 miles. Fill 'er up, sun!

# CAR-CRAZED CELEB
# LADY GAGA!

Lady Gaga is not just obsessed with music and fashion — she is also an all-out car nut. In an interview on The Zach Sang Show, she talked about why she loves old cars so much.

> I've got a slammed '65 Continental. It's like a boat mixed with a living room from the '60s. It's white with maroon interior and I can barely take it anywhere. It's like a museum piece! ... I've tried the fancy exotic car thing — I used to ride around in something modern and fancy and expensive and I just don't really love it. I'm not a speed person, I just want to feel cool while I'm driving it! So I'm a vintage car person, with maybe some new engines in them so I can drive farther.

↑ She goes gaga for vintage rides like this Lincoln Continental.

# ? DID YOU KNOW?

## A LONG TIME AGO, BLACK WAS THE FASTEST COLOR

You know that the Ford Model T was the first affordable car to be mass-produced on an assembly line. But maybe you didn't know that for 11 years, the cars only came in one color: black. The reason? Black paint dried faster than other colors. The quicker they could get them out of the factory, the faster they could sell them. Makes "cents" to us!

# FILL IN THE BLANKS
# I ACCIDENTALLY USED MY MOM'S TIME MACHINE!

Ask a friend for a word for each blank, but don't tell them what the story is about! Then read it back and get ready to laugh.

My mom is a super _____ scientist, and she always tells me to stay away from
　　　　　　　　　　ADJECTIVE

her inventions because they can be very_____ .
　　　　　　　　　　　　　　　　　　ADJECTIVE

One day I was down in my _____ basement and my pet _____
　　　　　　　　　　　　　ADJECTIVE　　　　　　　　　　　　　　ANIMAL

ran behind my mom's time machine. When I tried to get _____ to come out, I
　　　　　　　　　　　　　　　　　　　　　　　　　　PET NAME

accidentally hit the "on" button and sent both of us _____ years into the future!
　　　　　　　　　　　　　　　　　　　　　　　　NUMBER

There was a _____ flash of light, and when the door opened, I couldn't
　　　　　　　ADJECTIVE

believe my_____. My_____ town was gone and was
　　　　　　PLURAL BODY PART　　　　　ADJECTIVE

replaced by a _____ futuristic city!
　　　　　　　ADJECTIVE

Instead of grass and trees and_____, there were only machines, wires, and
　　　　　　　　　　　　　　PLURAL NOUN

beeping_____. And in the park, instead of kids playing, I only saw robots
　　　　　PLURAL NOUN

_____ -ing.
　VERB

When I saw one very_____ robot point his laser_____ at me, I knew
　　　　　　　　　ADJECTIVE　　　　　　　　　　　　NOUN

it was time to leave. Plus, I was getting hungry, and tonight my family always orders

_____ delivery. So we hopped back in the time machine, but I didn't know which
TYPE OF FOOD

_____ to press!
NOUN

Just when I thought we would be stuck in the future forever, _____ had an
　　　　　　　　　　　　　　　　　　　　　　　　　　SAME PET NAME

accident on the control panel. There was a _____ boom and when I opened my
　　　　　　　　　　　　　　　　　　　ADJECTIVE

eyes, we were back in my basement! I was so _____!
　　　　　　　　　　　　　　　　　　EMOTION

My mom was _____ to see us and asked what I thought of her time machine. I
　　　　　　　EMOTION

told her it was _____ , but I think it could use a bathroom.
　　　　　　　ADJECTIVE

# WHY DO CAR HORNS HONK?

Today honking a horn is usually a sign of being annoyed, but in the early days of automobiles, it was just the opposite. It was considered a nice thing to do, says Matt Anderson, curator for transportation at the Henry Ford museum. "You were expected to honk your horn if you were coming up on pedestrians, to let them know you were bounding down the street."

As for the sound, it's been an evolution. Anderson explains that in the early 1900s, there were three popular versions: a squeeze bulb, a horn that connected to the exhaust pipe which sounded like a steam locomotive, and an electric horn. Then an inventor named Miller Reese Hutchison came up with the Klaxon, which was used

in many Model T Fords, and had a unique "ahooga" sound that you hear in a lot of movies and TV shows that take place in the past.

These days, a company called Bosch supplies a lot of car companies with horns, including BMW, Chrysler, Fiat, Ford, General Motors, Honda, Mercedes-Benz, Porsche, Renault, Subaru, Volvo, and many others. And while technology allows horns to honk loudly and repeatedly, the law doesn't. In fact you can get a ticket for beeping too much. So much for being nice!

# WOOD YOU BELIEVE IT?

It may seem strange today, but for decades carmakers thought it was cool to stick wood on the sides of their cars!

The "woody" look has its roots in the early days of the automobile, when many of the first "horseless carriages" were made almost entirely of wood. Passenger compartments were often made by carpenters and furniture makers.

Eventually, automakers branched out (get it?) and started to use metal because of its strength and lower cost — plus

you don't have to worry about termites on a road trip.

Still, customers wanted the luxurious look of the wood-bodied cars. "Woody" wagons were especially popular with surfers during the 1960s, and family cars in the 1980s often sported fake wood stickers on the sides. Even the Chrysler PT Cruiser offered a

fake wood option until 2004.

While it's rare to see wood on cars today, many luxury brands stick to using wood on interior parts like dashboards, steering wheels, and shifters. So the next time you leave for school, imagine if your car looked like a treehouse!

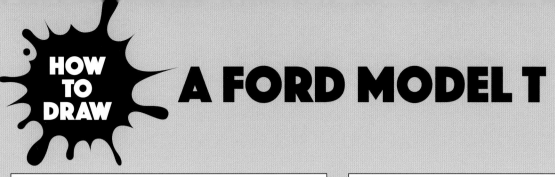

# HOW TO DRAW

# A FORD MODEL T

**1.** Start with two rectangles. They will become the car's cabin and front.

**2.** Get rolling! Give your ride a skinny set of tires.

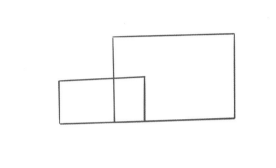

**3.** Round the roof, and for the car's grille and headlights, imagine drawing glasses and a little hat.

**4.** Draw lines in the cabin to create windows, then give the wheels spokes, and add lines to the body for engine vents.

**5.** Add fenders over the tires, a steering wheel, and a door.

**6.** Time for coloring!

# HELP, MY CAR IS HAUNTED

**Check out some freaky stories of haunted roads and rides.**

## HENRY FORD'S TIDY GHOST

In 1904, Henry Ford built the Piquette Avenue Plant in Detroit where the company first produced the famous Model T. These days, the building is a museum where visitors can see all kinds of cool relics from automotive history — and an occasional ghost! Local historian Bailey Sisoy-Moore, who leads tours through the museum, says she has seen a lot of strange things happen here, particularly in a re-creation of Henry Ford's office. Ford was an avid bird watcher during his life, and so the museum curators put a telescope in the office. They leave it pointed down at night, and many mornings, they find it pointed out the window! Also, Henry Ford was a super-busy guy, and his desk was usually covered in a jumble of papers. So one day, an education director at the museum decided to make the room all messy to mimic how it was in real life. And when she came back days later, everything was neatly stacked and organized! (Hey, ghost of Henry Ford, would you mind cleaning our room, too?)

## JAMES DEAN'S EVIL PORSCHE

In 1955, super-famous actor James Dean tragically died in a car accident while driving his beloved Porsche 550 Spyder. The car was totaled and sent to a salvage yard. Two car-obsessed doctors pulled parts from Dean's trashed car to use in their own rides, and both of them got into terrible accidents! The frame and shell of the car were taken by the National Safety Council and sent out on a tour to promote safe driving. While in storage, the car mysteriously burst into flames but weirdly sustained very little damage. The Porsche also fell off a display stand and hurt a bystander. A bunch more bad stuff happened with this car, but honestly, we're getting a little freaked out. Let's move on!

## GHOST BUSSER

On the streets of Philadelphia, legend has it that there is a Southeastern Pennsylvania Transportation Authority bus that cruises the streets late at night with no known destination. "The Wandering Bus," as it is called, supposedly only appears when you truly need it. And here's the super-weird part: They say that when you climb aboard, you can ride as long as you want, but once your feet touch the pavement as you get off, all memories about the bus and any other passengers on it disappear. The legend says that some

**Actor James Dean cruising in his soon-to-be cursed Porsche 550 Spyder.**

people stay onboard for days or even years. That sounds incredibly bizarre and boring at the same time.

## KNOCK KNOCK, WHO'S THERE?

Staying out super-late in Detroit can have some super-creepy results. According to one legend, if you're driving on Strasburg Road and no one is around, you might not want to stay at a stop sign too long. Some drivers have said that while stopped, they see a little girl emerge from the shadows. She stares at the driver with deep, dark eyes. Drivers look away, and a split-second later, there is a knock knock on the driver's side window and the little girl is right there! Then she disappears back into the night. What does this little girl want? We're not sticking around to ask!

## UH-OH, WHAT'S THAT GLOW?

On Chena Hot Springs Road in Fairbanks, Alaska, locals say that between miles 8 and 12, this road is regularly haunted by blue, white, and orange orbs of light. Witnesses say they look like headlights floating in the sky, and sometimes they even follow cars. Maybe it's an alien spaceship looking for directions to the mall?

## BAD VIBES BRIDGE

There are a lot of stories about the Charles Burr Lane Bridge in Louisiana — and none of them are normal! Some drivers have reported seeing the ghost of an old man holding a lantern. Others have said that while driving, they get the sense that they're not alone and, after looking in the rearview mirror,

see an outlined shadow of a person sitting in the back seat. Another driver said they've heard mysterious drums. Maybe the lantern guy and the dude in the back seat have a band together?

## SPOOK HILL HELPERS

Spook Hill is a freaky road in Maryland that is near the site of the Civil War Battle of Antietam. People say that if you put your car in neutral at the bottom of the hill, your car will roll up it. Some say it's the ghosts of soldiers who believe they are still at war and are pushing cannons. Science has another explanation: Spook Hill is something called a "gravity hill," which is an optical illusion that can trick the eye into thinking a downward slope is going uphill. So not so scary, but still pretty weird!

# PERFORMANCE CAR OF THE YEAR FLASHBACK

PCOTY (short for Performance Car of the Year) is an annual contest where *Road & Track* magazine tests the newest models of the world's most incredible supercars and declares a winner based on their speed, handling, comfort, and overall awesomeness. Check out this lineup of the best of the best from every year since the contest first revved its engine.

### 2013 CHEVROLET CORVETTE STINGRAY

In the first year of PCOTY, the then-new seventh-generation Vette beat amazing Porsches and Ferraris with its power, speed, ease of handling, and for the first time in Corvette history, super-comfy seats!

### 2015 PORSCHE 911 GT3

From the racetrack to the streets, the Porsche 911 GT3 wowed the judges with its crazy quickness, sweet looks, and the option for a concert-quality stereo (which could either be great or terrible, depending on who is picking the music).

### 2016 FORD MUSTANG SHELBY GT350R

With an engine that revs past 8000 rpm and can hit a top speed of 174 mph, the GT350R zoomed past its competition faster than you can say ... well, anything, really.

## 2017 ACURA NSX

Shutting down tough competition from powerhouse rides like the Lotus Evora 400 and the Corvette Grand Sport, the Acura NSX is PCOTY's first hybrid winner. High-tech instrumentation and old-school awesomeness live together under one hood. Isn't that sweet?

## 2018 MCLAREN 720S

In a rush? This ride is for you. It hits 62 mph in 2.8 seconds and 124 mph in 7.8 seconds!

## 2019 CHEVROLET CORVETTE ZR1

The most powerful Corvette ever made, its massive supercharged V-8 puts out 755 hp. You'll hear it coming long before you see it!

## 2020 HYUNDAI VELOSTER N

How did a $30,000 hatchback beat supercars like the Lamborghini Huracán Evo? Because it exhibits the essence of what this contest is all about: It is incredibly fun to drive!

## 2021 FORD MUSTANG SHELBY GT500

This thing eats racetracks for lunch, and then has a bowl of winding mountain roads for dessert. On any surface in any condition, it is an absolute demon.

**1930s**
Two racers decide to play leapfrog during a Sprint Car race on a dirt track.

**1920s**
AG Miller revs up his Wolseley single-seater race car in England. That "helmet" does not look very protective!

# THE ROARING TWENTIES, THIRTIES, AND FORTIES

## AS LONG AS THERE HAVE BEEN CARS, THERE HAVE BEEN RACES! CHECK OUT SOME OF THE COOLEST SPEED MACHINES AND WILDEST SMASHUPS EVER.

**1938**
Dick Seaman pilots his Mercedes during the Donington Grand Prix in 1938. Who needs a windshield when you have super-dorky goggles?

**1940s**
"Hey, who put this fence in the middle of the racetrack?" asks driver Billy Carden at the Macon Fairgrounds Speedway.

**1940s**
The driver of this car is named Fonty Flock. Did you expect someone with that name to drive well?

**1928**
Kurt C. Volkhart takes his rocket car out for a joyride to the moon.

**1920s**
J.G. Parry-Thomas tests his car "Babs" as he prepares to break a record. (Record for the weirdest looking car, we're guessing.)

**1938**
This is either the car that British racing driver John Cobb used to break the world land speed record in 1938 or it is evidence that UFOs are real.

**1937**
Confused by what's going on in this photo? That's okay, the driver has no clue what's happening either.

**1948**
Two piles of hay play catch with a full-size race car.

# THE UNITED STATES OF
# WACKY CAR LAWS

**OREGON**
If you leave your car door open too long, you're leaving yourself open to getting a fine.

**MONTANA**
Unless you have a chaperone, it's illegal to have sheep in your truck bed. (Sounds like a *baaaad* idea.)

**KANSAS**
No squealing in Kansas: Tire burnouts have been banned in this state.

**ALASKA**
It is illegal to tie a dog to a car roof way up north. Sorry Scruffy, you'll have to stick your head out the window like all the other dogs.

**TEXAS**
You are required to have windshield wipers, but oddly, you aren't required to have a windshield.

**OKLAHOMA**
Batman usually fights criminals, but in Oklahoma, he can land you in the slammer! It's a crime to read a comic book while driving here.

**MISSISSIPPI**
In Oxford, you're going to need to press the mute button on your horn — it's illegal to honk, because you might scare a horse.

# HONK IF YOU THINK THESE REAL-LIFE ROAD RULES ARE REALLY WEIRD!

**ILLINOIS**
Sorry, it's illegal to drive a car without a steering wheel. Apparently, being able to turn a car is very, very important.

**TENNESSEE**
Note to hunters in Tennessee zipping down the highway: You can't shoot any game from a moving vehicle.

**MASSACHUSETTS**
Here's a fun way to get pulled over by the police: Drive with a gorilla in your backseat.

**OHIO**
Make sure you fill up, because it's against the law to run out of gas in Youngstown.

**DELAWARE**
It is illegal to change clothes in your vehicle. So don't you dare switch from soccer cleats to baseball cleats on the way to the game!

**SOUTH CAROLINA**
You're not allowed to store trash in a vehicle in Hilton Head. Hope the cops don't see how messy our backseat floor is!

**GEORGIA**
It's illegal to spit from a car or bus. How are we supposed to have fun on field trips then?

**ALABAMA**
You are not allowed to drive while blindfolded. Darn, that really messes up our plans to play Pin the Tail on the Donkey in a Ferrari.

**FLORIDA**
You must feed a parking meter if you tie an alligator to it. (Just don't feed the parking meter to the alligator.)

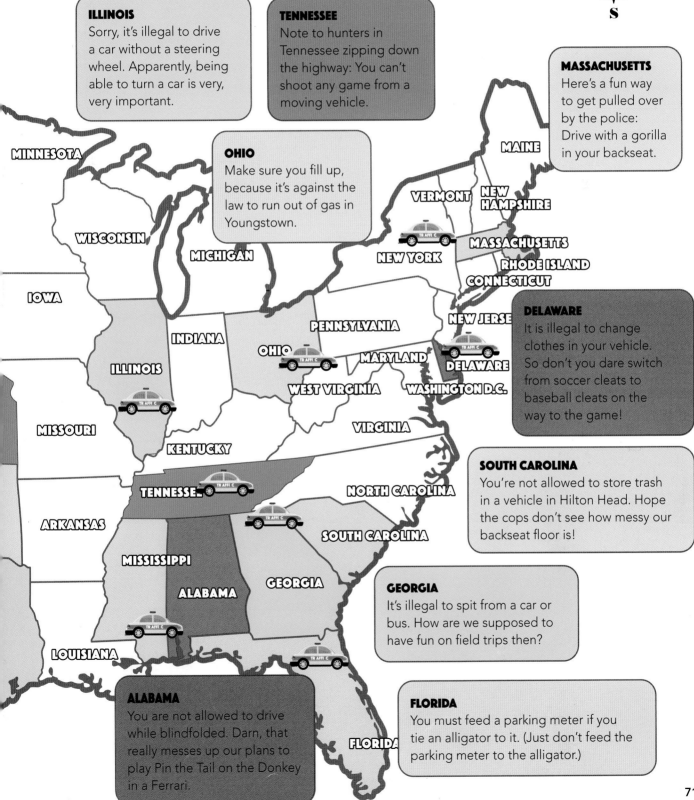

# THE RAREST RIDE ON EARTH

There are many incredible things you should know about this 1962 Ferrari 250 GTO. We'll start with the fact that only 36 were ever made. Then we'll mention that it came in first place at the 1962 Italian GT Championship. Then we'll let you know that Ferrari engineers dubbed it Il Mostro — the monster — because of its strange looks and that if you wanted to buy one, you needed to be personally approved by Ferrari's founder, Enzo Ferrari. And finally, we'll mention that it is the most expensive car ever sold at auction.

IN 2018, RM SOTHEBY'S SOLD IT FOR $48.4 MILLION!

# WHICH DRIVER FROM HISTORY ARE YOU?

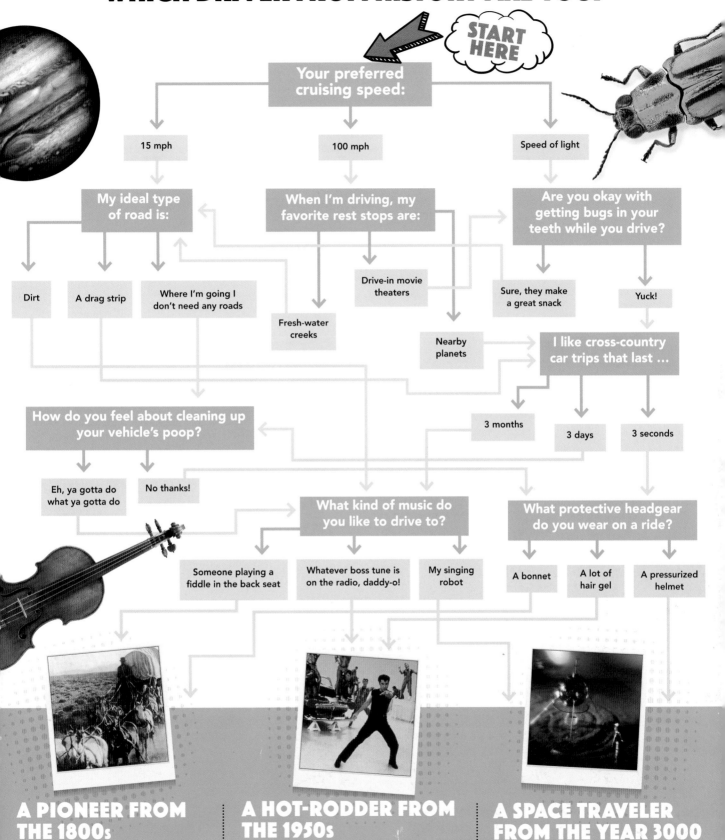

**START HERE**

**Your preferred cruising speed:**

- 15 mph
- 100 mph
- Speed of light

**My ideal type of road is:**
- Dirt
- A drag strip
- Where I'm going I don't need any roads

**When I'm driving, my favorite rest stops are:**
- Fresh-water creeks
- Drive-in movie theaters
- Nearby planets

**Are you okay with getting bugs in your teeth while you drive?**
- Sure, they make a great snack
- Yuck!

**I like cross-country car trips that last …**
- 3 months
- 3 days
- 3 seconds

**How do you feel about cleaning up your vehicle's poop?**
- Eh, ya gotta do what ya gotta do
- No thanks!

**What kind of music do you like to drive to?**
- Someone playing a fiddle in the back seat
- Whatever boss tune is on the radio, daddy-o!
- My singing robot

**What protective headgear do you wear on a ride?**
- A bonnet
- A lot of hair gel
- A pressurized helmet

## A PIONEER FROM THE 1800s
Heading to California in search of gold? Good thing your rickety covered wagon has plenty of trunk space!

## A HOT-RODDER FROM THE 1950s
You're a perfect fit for a time when cars looked and sounded like absolute beasts. The downside? No Spotify or YouTube for long trips.

## A SPACE TRAVELER FROM THE YEAR 3000
Quick, find (or invent) a time machine. The 21st century is way too slow for your tastes.

73

"Outta the way, I'm late for the sandcastle-building contest!"

CHAPTER 4

# STYLE
# & DESIGN

# LOOKS THAT THRILL!

They say that a great work of art can move you to tears. And in the case of automotive art, it can also move you to the drive-thru window to pick up your burger and fries! When it comes to amazing car design, it isn't as easy as just making them look cool — there are all kinds of things engineers need to consider to make them more comfortable, more fuel-efficient and, of course, faster. Check out all of the hard work that goes into making vehicles look as amazing as they perform.

**BUGATTI (PRONOUNCED BOO-GOT-TEE)**

**ONE VERY LUCKY AND VERY RICH CAR NUT RECENTLY BOUGHT A ONE-OF-A-KIND BUGATTI SUPERCAR FOR $18.9 MILLION, MAKING IT THE MOST EXPENSIVE NEW CAR EVER SOLD!**

## SOME TERMS YOU'LL SEE THROUGHOUT THIS CHAPTER:

| | |
|---|---|
| **COUPE** | Sporty car with a sloping roofline and two doors. |
| **ICONIC** | The ultimate, perfect example. |
| **LOGO** | A symbol that represents a company. |
| **SUSPENSION** | The system of tires, springs, and shock absorbers that work together to give vehicles stability — and passengers a comfy ride. |
| **T-TOP** | A car roof that has removable panels on each side of a bar that runs down the middle of the roof. |

# hot rod heaven

Some sculptors work with chisels and marble, others with welding torches and sheetmetal. Paul Martinez, who runs *Rodding USA* magazine, tells us all about building one-of-a-kind car creations called hot rods.

### What is a hot rod?

The Merriam-Webster dictionary defines a hot rod as an automobile rebuilt or modified for high speed and fast acceleration. My definition goes beyond speed to include the car's look, its stance, and the owner's passion. Hot-rodding began in the late 1930s in Southern California when car enthusiasts would modify their cars and then go race them on the dry lakes located northeast of Los Angeles.

### What's the difference between a hot rod and a street rod?

Street rods are from before and up to 1948. They tend to keep more of the body's original/stock look with modified suspension, engine, transmission, and interior creature comforts. They get painted any color of the rainbow and always have custom wheels.

### How long does it take to build a hot rod?

A home-built hot rod might take two to 10 years, while one built at a professional shop could be done in a year or so. It all depends on the car's condition and the number of modifications.

### How fast do they go?

Depending on the engine and the body, I've seen them run 200 mph on the Bonneville Salt Flats in Utah!

### Can you take them to a drive-thru?

Typically when you go through a drive-thru in a hot rod, you have to shut the car off so you can hear the voice on the speaker. It's always fun to see the cashier's reaction when you pull up and they see what you are driving!

## HOT ROD MUST-HAVES

Some of the defining characteristics that make hot rods so awesome.

**CHOP** Cutting the roof's height makes the car more aerodynamic and adds some cool factor.

**CHANNEL** By cutting out the floor and rewelding it higher into the body, it lowers the car.

**STANCE** The attitude is achieved by modifying the suspension and using a smaller tire in front and a larger one in the rear.

**ENGINE** The original hot rods were powered by modified stock flathead V-8 engines. The introduction of the Chevrolet V-8 in 1955 made it a popular choice because of the amount of horsepower it produced.

**LOUVERS** Found on the tops and sides of the hood and the trunk lid, they allow heat to escape from the engine.

**FLAMES** Hot-rod flames typically start with yellow or white and end in orange or red.

**1932 FORD 5-WINDOW COUPE**

**1934 FORD 3-WINDOW COUPE**

**1940 FORD COUPE**

**1932 FORD ROADSTER**

**SOME OF PAUL'S FAVORITE HOT RODS**

**1934 FORD 5-WINDOW COUPE**

# THE STORY BEHIND THE SYMBOL

Check out the surprising meanings of some of the most famous hood ornaments and car logos.

## AUDI

The four silver rings symbolize the 1932 merger of four German car manufacturers into one: Audi, DKW, Horch, and Wanderer.

## HYUNDAI

The "H" represents the Brand name and is designed to look like two people shaking hands. The oval represents perpetual motion.

## BMW

Called "the BMW Roundel," the blue-and-white panels represent the flag of Bavaria, a region in Germany that is connected to the luxury automaker.

## LAMBORGHINI

Founder Ferruccio Lamborghini visited a ranch and was in such awe of the fighting bulls he saw that he adopted their look as his company's emblem.

## CHEVROLET

There are a few versions of how Chevy's "bow tie" was designed. One is that William C. Durant, co-founder of General Motors and Chevrolet, copied it from the pattern on a hotel's wallpaper.

## FERRARI

Enzo Ferrari met the parents of a fighter pilot who had a prancing horse painted on his plane. Enzo was told the symbol was good luck, so he decided to use it on his cars and added a yellow background to represent the town of Modena, Italy, where the Ferrari factory was located.

## CADILLAC

Cadillac is the last name of the man who founded the city of Detroit, Michigan, in 1701. This emblem is an interpretation of the Cadillac family coat of arms, which had trios of birds and a black bar that were symbols used by knights. The red band stands for boldness.

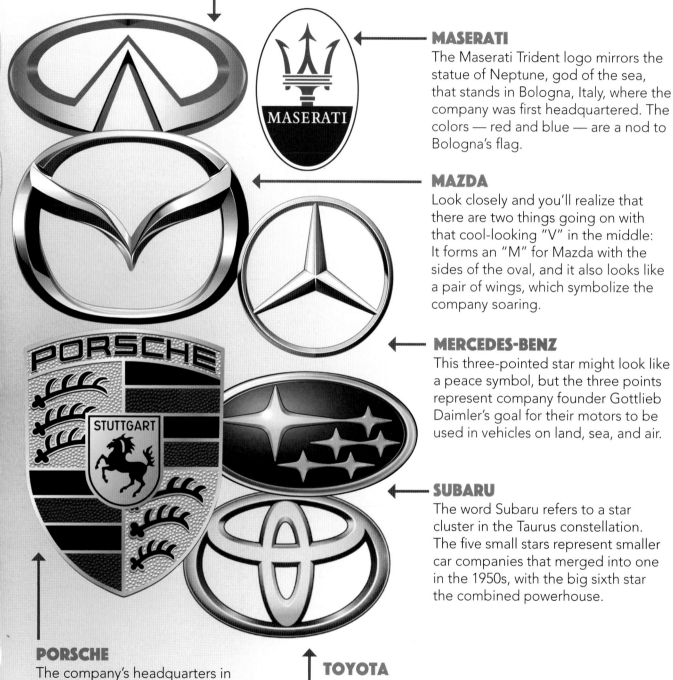

### INFINITI
What you're looking at is an oval surrounding a road that gets narrow as it disappears into the distance. To Infiniti . . . and beyond!

### MASERATI
The Maserati Trident logo mirrors the statue of Neptune, god of the sea, that stands in Bologna, Italy, where the company was first headquartered. The colors — red and blue — are a nod to Bologna's flag.

### MAZDA
Look closely and you'll realize that there are two things going on with that cool-looking "V" in the middle: It forms an "M" for Mazda with the sides of the oval, and it also looks like a pair of wings, which symbolize the company soaring.

### MERCEDES-BENZ
This three-pointed star might look like a peace symbol, but the three points represent company founder Gottlieb Daimler's goal for their motors to be used in vehicles on land, sea, and air.

### SUBARU
The word Subaru refers to a star cluster in the Taurus constellation. The five small stars represent smaller car companies that merged into one in the 1950s, with the big sixth star the combined powerhouse.

### PORSCHE
The company's headquarters in Stuttgart, Germany, was built on the former grounds of a horse farm, which is why there is a horse so prominently featured in the logo. The antlers and the red-and-black stripes represent the old kingdom of which Stuttgart was the capital.

### TOYOTA
You see those three ovals? They kind of look like a T, and for Toyota, they represent three important things: the hearts of their customers, their cars, and future innovation.

# COOL JOB ALERT!

## HOT WHEELS DESIGNER

### MEET LINDSEY LEE, WHO BUILDS AND PLAYS WITH TOYS FOR A LIVING!

**Wait, your job is designing Hot Wheels? Can you hear our readers freaking out right now?**
Yes! This is the best job in the world, I freak out every single day. I mean, I get to design cars and work with the no.1 selling toy in the world.

**What were your favorite subjects in school?**
Lunch … but if I need to pick something academic, I would say art or history class. History was the class that challenged me the most, while art class allowed me to unleash my experimental side and relieve stress.

**Did you always want to be a designer?**
I've always loved to draw, but I never thought that I would become a designer. My passion for designing came later as I took art courses in college and honed my skills through the learning process, challenges and accomplishments. Challenge accepted!

**What advice would you give to kids who would love to design cars and toys?**
Becoming a designer requires observation, so my advice would be to observe everything and anything, both as a whole and in detail. If you want to become a car designer, observe cars and other mechanical parts.

BATMAN

**ROCKIN' SANTA SLED**

**What is your favorite Hot Wheels car you've worked on?**
I love all of my Hot Wheels designs, but I would say the Rockin' Santa Sled is one of my favorites. Working on that design allowed me to learn more about the Rolamatic wheel, which is a special type of wheel system. Plus, it is a fun car for the holidays that also looks super sleek!

**What's more important in your opinion: speed or looks?**
Both speed and looks are extremely important in the auto world. It is both legendary design and epic performance that's allowed Hot Wheels to prove our influence on car culture. However as a designer, I'd have to say looks are most important. The beauty of design is that we are able to make a "slow" car look fast just by adjusting the looks.

**How long is the process from initial design to finished product?**
It varies by car, but when it is all said and done, it takes roughly 10-12 months. Other steps in the process once design is complete are manufacturing and packaging.

**Do you get in trouble at work for NOT playing with cars?**
Well, luckily I always play with cars so I wouldn't know!

# CHECK OUT LINDSEY'S COOLEST CARS!

**FORD RANGER RAPTOR**

**PORSCHE PANAMERA**

**CAPTAIN AMERICA**

**NEMO**

**JAR JAR BINKS**

**MICKEY MOUSE**

# WHICH SUPERSTAR DRIVES

See if you can match the car-obsessed celeb to their favorite stylin' rides.

**A** JOHN CENA

**B** KEVIN HART

**C** LADY GAGA

**D** TOM BRADY

**E** BEYONCÉ

**F** LEBRON JAMES

**G** MANNY PACQUIAO

**H** KYLIE JENNER

**I** JUSTIN BIEBER

# WHICH SUPERCAR?

1. **FERRARI 458 ITALIA**
2. **FERRARI LAFERRARI**
3. **PORSCHE 911 TURBO S**
4. **LAMBORGHINI AVENTADOR COUPE**
5. **ASTON MARTIN DB11**
6. **LIGHT-BLUE FORD BRONCO**
7. **1971 PLYMOUTH ROAD RUNNER**
8. **MERCEDES-BENZ SLR MCLAREN**
9. **FORD MUSTANG GT500E**

Check out the answers on page 140!

# THIS CLAY ISN'T FOR PLAY!

We live in an age of amazing computer technology, but when **Mark Trostle**, head of design for Ram Trucks and Mopar, gets a great idea he wants to try out, he turns to a giant, life-size lump of clay. Here's why.

### Why design cars with clay?
A car is a sculpture — a sculpture that happens to do a lot of things like drive! And as good as digital technology is at making designing more efficient, we still want to be able to touch the model. Clay is a great way for us to be able to change and manipulate the way the car looks until we get it right.

### What kind of clay do you use?
Different types are used throughout the automotive industry. The one we use is called America Art Clay. It is automotive grade and has Georgia red clay in it. We heat the clay because it's pretty hard in its natural state.

### What's the process like?
The model starts with an aluminum platform that has real wheels. On top of that, we put an armature, which is a kind of frame, and foam blocks cut in the shape of the vehicle. The sculptor then applies the clay over that and uses different tools, like scrapers and rakes and milling machines, to fine-tune the shape.

### How do you test your designs?
We put a kind of film over the clay that allows us to paint the vehicle so we can look at reflections, highlights, and things like that. And we spend a lot of time in wind tunnels making sure that the vehicle's shape allows it to cut through the air while being fuel efficient.

### How much clay do you use in a year?
We use 12,000 pounds of clay a year creating designs for Ram, Dodge, Chrysler, and Jeep brands.

### What happens to the models when you're done?
We keep them in storage because we can reuse them when we want to make different types of updates to the vehicle. Cut off the front end or put more clay to alter the hood — that kind of thing. And then in some cases, we have stripped off all the clay from the models and donated it to design universities that do clay modeling.

### When you see vehicles on the road, do you wish you could take your scraper and reshape the ugly parts?
Absolutely! I always do. That's the fun part of my job as a designer, having art and science work together to create a neat-looking and high-functioning vehicle.

Mark Trostle

# FUNNY NAME GAME

### ALL OF THESE STRANGE CAR NAMES ARE REAL — EXCEPT ONE. CAN YOU FIND THE FAKE?

**MITSUBISHI MINICA LETTUCE**

**ISUZU MYSTERIOUS UTILITY WIZARD**

**TOYOTA DELIBOY**

**AMC GREMLIN**

**MAZDA BONGO FRIENDEE**

**FORD FLIPPER**

Check out the answer on page 140!

# DRIVING IN DISGUISE

**Want to know how automakers test their latest cars without revealing the new designs to everyone on the road?**
They dress their cars in disguises! Sound crazy? Well, it's true. When manufacturers are designing and testing cars, they build "development mules" that they wrap in special camouflage, hiding the shape of the grille, the windows — even the roofline.

"A new car design takes several years and millions of [dollars] to develop, and it is very important that camouflage is used to keep the design as secret as possible," explains Adam Hatton, exterior design director at Jaguar. "It protects the initial 'wow' factor and freshness to market of a new car, which adds to customer desirability. It also helps prevent new design ideas being potentially copied by other companies."

Sometimes they might even print fake headlights, or tape on random plastic parts just to hide what the actual car looks like underneath. "You can make a coupe design look like a wagon by adding hard plastic camouflage to the rear. Fake window shapes and lamp shapes are always good to do, too," says Hatton.

It takes a lot of effort to keep a prototype car secret, but carmakers think that revealing a brand new car design should be a big surprise.

**CAN YOU IDENTIFY THESE CARS UNDER THEIR TEST CAMOUFLAGE?**

**Check out the answers on page 140!**

# LEGEND OF
# LAMBOR

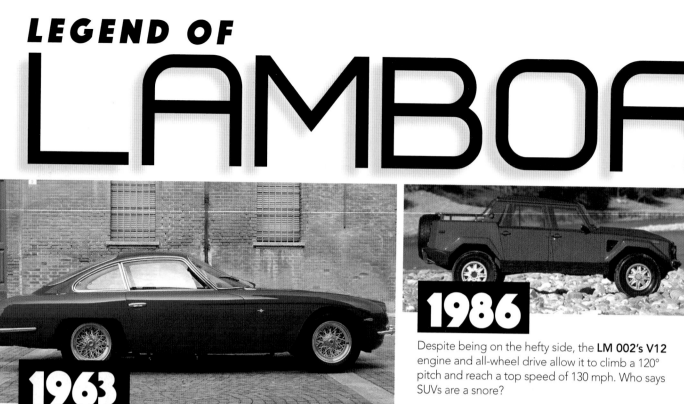

## 1986

Despite being on the hefty side, the **LM 002's V12** engine and all-wheel drive allow it to climb a 120° pitch and reach a top speed of 130 mph. Who says SUVs are a snore?

## 1963

Tractor factory owner **Ferruccio Lamborghini** decides to start a company in Italy that will build the greatest cars the world has ever seen. Lambo's first model, the 350 GT, rolls out and almost causes an earthquake when everyone's jaws hit the ground at once.

## 1973

The **Countach's** fascinating and unconventional shape hits the Geneva Motor Show. We feel really bad for whatever boring car was parked next to it.

## 1966

Lamborghini reveals the **Miura**, which is the name of a kind of fighting bull. At the time, it was the fastest production car ever made. How do you say "speeding ticket" in Italian?

## 1976

The **Silhouette** has a detachable roof that could be stored behind its seats. Don't lose that roof — only 53 were ever made!

# GHINI

Take a speedy trip down memory lane with the most stylish supercar company of them all.

## 2015

A rear-wheel-drive wonder, the **Huracán RWD** goes back to basics. Lambo says it is their most fun car to drive. C'mon, is any Lambo not fun to drive?

## 2001

In collaboration with Audi, Lambo designers came up with the **Murciélago**, a 580-hp beast named after the Spanish word for bat. "Can I have one, pretty please?" asked Batman.

## 1990

The **Diablo** roars to life. The bosses at Lamborghini wished for a car that had a maximum speed of at least 198 mph, and the Diablo granted that wish with a top speed of 200 mph.

## 2011

The unique design and innovative technological package of the **Aventador LP 700-4** brings an impossibly high standard to future supercar design and function. (Just like that kid in class who always gets straight As and never gets in trouble.)

## 2021

Lamborghini announces that all of its models will be plug-in hybrids within three years. Charge!

# WHEEL-Y COOL WHEELS

Which rims belong to which ride? Check out the answers on page 140!

**A.**

**1.** BMW M2 COMPETITION

**B.**

**2.** CHEVROLET CAMARO 1LE

**C.**

**3.** MERCEDES AMG GT 4-DOOR

**D.**

**4.** HONDA CIVIC TYPE R

**E.**

**5.** PORSCHE GT3 RS

# A LAMBORGHINI

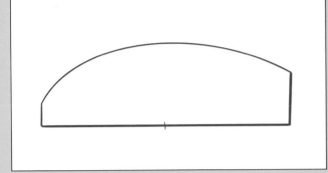

**1.** Draw a rectangle with a slightly longer side on the back and connect with a curved line.

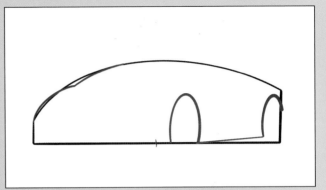

**2.** Add two half ovals for the tire wells.

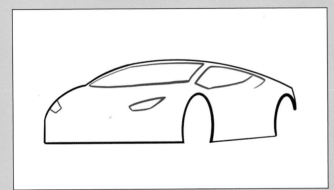

**3.** Put in windshield and headlights.

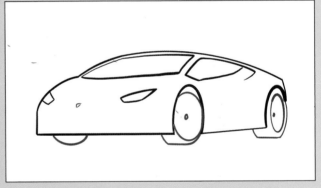

**4.** Add some fat tires.

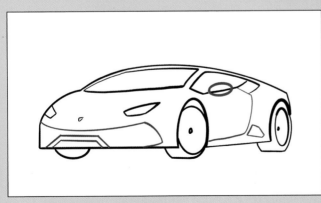

**5.** Give it a door and grill.

**6.** Color and smoke those wheels!

# WHICH CAR PAINT JOB MATCHES YOUR PERSONALITY?

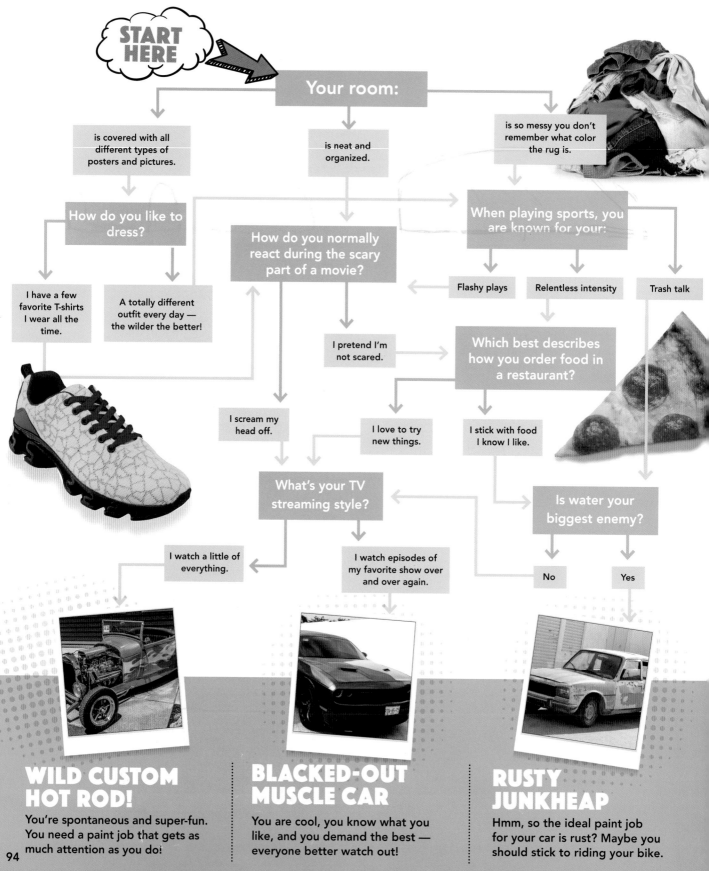

**START HERE**

**Your room:**

- is covered with all different types of posters and pictures.
- is neat and organized.
- is so messy you don't remember what color the rug is.

**How do you like to dress?**

- I have a few favorite T-shirts I wear all the time.
- A totally different outfit every day — the wilder the better!

**How do you normally react during the scary part of a movie?**

- I pretend I'm not scared.
- I scream my head off.

**When playing sports, you are known for your:**

- Flashy plays
- Relentless intensity
- Trash talk

**Which best describes how you order food in a restaurant?**

- I love to try new things.
- I stick with food I know I like.

**What's your TV streaming style?**

- I watch a little of everything.
- I watch episodes of my favorite show over and over again.

**Is water your biggest enemy?**

- No
- Yes

## WILD CUSTOM HOT ROD!
You're spontaneous and super-fun. You need a paint job that gets as much attention as you do!

## BLACKED-OUT MUSCLE CAR
You are cool, you know what you like, and you demand the best — everyone better watch out!

## RUSTY JUNKHEAP
Hmm, so the ideal paint job for your car is rust? Maybe you should stick to riding your bike.

# WHAT'S THE MOST
# POPULAR CAR COLOR?

See if you can put these colors in order from most popular to least popular.

1. _____ 2. _____ 3. _____ 4. _____ 5. _____ 6. _____

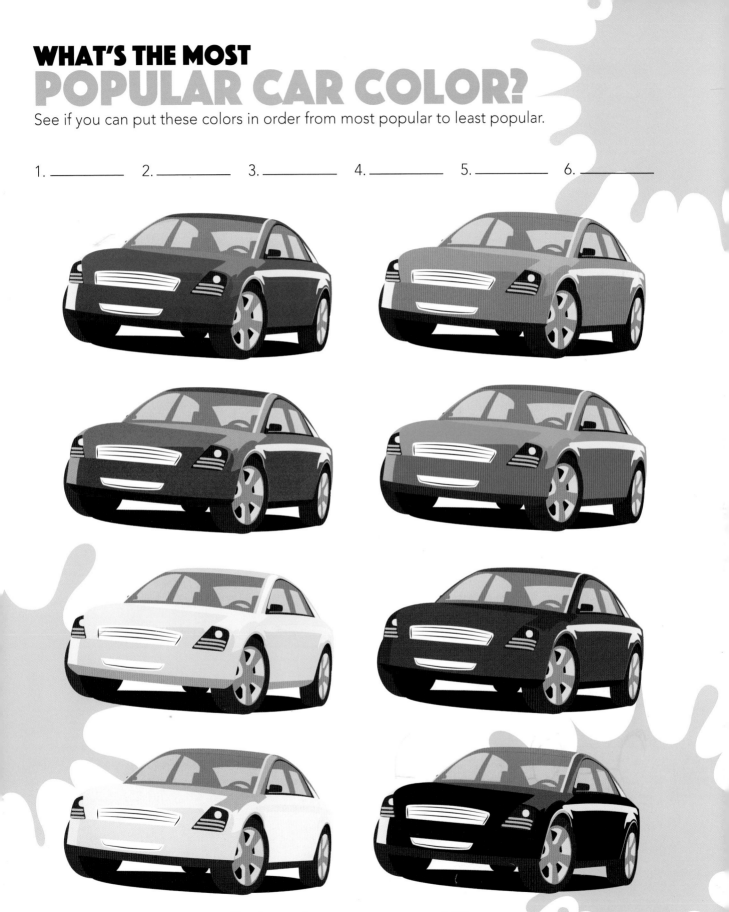

**Check out the answers on page 140!**

"Is now a good time to mention that I'm scared of heights?"

# CHAPTER 5

# SCREEN MACHINES

## COOLEST CARS FROM MOVIES, TV & GAMING

# LIGHTS, CAMERA, ACTION!

Lightning McQueen is one of the most famous car characters in movie history. (Don't ask him for his autograph, he's very busy. Plus, he doesn't have hands to hold a pen.) Read on to learn about some of the coolest vehicles ever to cruise across a screen in movies, TV, and gaming.

"LIGHTYEAR" TIRES ARE A TRIBUTE TO BUZZ LIGHTYEAR, AND NUMBER 95 REFERS TO 1995, THE YEAR *TOY STORY* WAS RELEASED.

**LIGHTNING MCQUEEN IS NOT BASED ON ANY EXISTING CARS, BUT HE DOES HAVE OFFICIAL SPECS: HE HAS A V-8 ENGINE, 750 HP, IS REAR-WHEEL DRIVE, HAS A TOP SPEED OF 200 MPH, AND CAN GO 0 TO 60 MPH IN 4.5 SECONDS.**

## SOME TERMS YOU'LL SEE THROUGHOUT THIS CHAPTER:

| | |
|---|---|
| **BIG-BLOCK V-8** | Chevy engines whose large size helped them produce more power. |
| **ENGINEERS** | Scientists who invent, design, analyze, and test machines, programs, and gadgets. |
| **REAR-WHEEL DRIVE** | The engine powers the rear tires only, which helps it accelerate more quickly than front-wheel drive. |
| **SPECS** | A list of important details about a car, its components, and how it performs. |
| **SUPER SPORT** | Chevys with an "SS" badge have high-performance tires, heavy-duty suspension, increased power, and special style accents. |

# HOW TO CRASH A

**Stephen A. Pope** is a stunt coordinator who has worked on a ton of movies and TV shows, including *The Avengers: Infinity War.* Here he breaks down the fine art of flipping, smashing, and bashing vehicles. LIGHTS, CAMERA, OUCH!

## SAFETY FIRST

"Safety is our priority. I will go through the script with the movie's director and producers to see what action we'll be filming, and if there is a scene where an actor needs to run through traffic, I will make sure we have expert drivers in those cars so there is no danger of them getting hit. Or if a scene involves a crash, we know we will need to add things inside the cars like protective roll cages or five-point harnesses, depending on how big the crash needs to be."

## BREAK OUT THE TOYS

"When we're going to do a big sequence, the movie's art department will print out a big overhead map of where we'll be shooting. Then we sit down with little Matchbox cars and plan out all of the action. We figure out where the cameras will need to be and — if the car is going to crash into a Dumpster, for example — we plan where it will be located and where a ramp could be hidden if we want the car to flip over."

## TAKE IT SLOW

"People who visit a film set during a driving stunt day are surprised to see how slow the cars are actually driving. We're usually not going faster than 25 to 30 mph, but the editing and camera angles might make it look like the car is going 90. That is for safety and to keep things in control."

## BREAK OUT THE CALCULATOR

"If we want the car to fly into the air, we use a device called a pipe ramp. Depending on the size of the vehicle and what you want it to do — flip over, land on its side, spin around as it launches — the pipe ramp will vary in size and angle. And again, even for some amazing stunts like you see in the *Fast & Furious* series, the car might hit the ramp only going 20 mph."

## YES, IT IS WEIRD TO GET IN AN ACCIDENT ON PURPOSE

"It's completely backward thinking, to intentionally crash. People look at what you do and say, 'That's crazy!' But when you're in the car, you just think through the plan, know that you have the proper safety gear, trust that the other drivers know what they are doing, and you're good to go. It's like playing football. You're nervous until you take that first hit, and then you settle down and do what you need to do."

# CAR ON PURPOSE

FAST & FURIOUS 9: THIS CAR DOESN'T NEED A PROPELLER TO FLY!

# COOL
## JOB ALERT!
# MOVIE CAR DESIGNER

Fireball **Tim Lawrence** is an amazing artist who has designed cars, boats, planes, and spaceships for about 400 movies, including *Batman, Jurassic Park, The Avengers,* and *Austin Powers.* We got him to slam the brakes on his drawing pencil and take a few minutes to answer our questions.

**How did you get started designing cars for movies?**

I went to the ArtCenter College of Design and answered an ad at school that said "Design a Movie Car!" Little did I know that the sketches I sent in would end up being the design for the Batmobile in the 1989 *Batman* film. From then on, with the help of my mentor, Syd Mead, I was hooked.

**How do you come up with such cool-looking ideas?**

As an artist, you have to trust those ideas that bubble up inside you. For the Batmobile, "intimidation" was the key to the design. It needed to scare the bejesus out of the Joker!

**What's the process like for designing a movie car?**

I get a script from the movie studio, I make notes on what it needs to do, and then I just start sketching like a madman! Sometimes I make hundreds of sketches. Then I add color with

markers and scan everything into the computer to finish and add the flash.

**What is something about movie cars that most people don't know?**

That they are just like actors! They can be easy to work with or temperamental. They can be calm and cool or throw a tantrum. In either case, you just have to be patient and tell them that they are doing a good job!

**What's it like when you see one of your drawings come to life?**

Oh, it's the best thing ever. Going to the movies and watching people's faces as a car jumps a bridge and knowing you were a big part of that? It's very rewarding.

**Which of your designs do you wish you got to keep in your driveway?**

That's a tough one, but certainly the Batmobile. I don't

think anyone's driveway is big enough for it, though. The muscle car I designed for *Son of the Mask* was awesome, too. It was a Holden Monaro V-8 from Australia, and it was fast!

**What was your favorite subject in school?**

Art was always my favorite in school, but at home, my parents were very good at feeding my passion. I always got die-cast cars like Hot Wheels, Matchbox, Dinkys, and Corgis, and art supplies for birthdays and Christmases. I still do! There's nothing else I really want. Creative expression brings me the most joy, and I'll do it forever.

**What is your advice to kids who hope to design cars one day?**

Start now. Start today doing what you love. Start and don't stop. Ever.

KNIGHT RIDER MUSTANG CONCEPT
©2008 Fireball Tim Entertainment
www.fireballtim.com
/CINEMA VEHICLE SERVICES/

MASK 2

MASK 2/ROAD RUNNER/VER..
©2003 FireballTim

BATMAN

©1986 Fireball Tim

(From upper left) Storyboard keyframe for *Jurassic Park*; KITT concept drawing for *Knight Rider* reboot; muscle car from *Son of The Mask*; storyboards for *The Lost World: Jurassic Park*; Batmobile sketch from 1989 *Batman* movie.

# ON YOUR MARK, GET SET, MARIO!

## The inside story of how designers created the 15th version of the most iconic video game vehicle ever.

Since 1992, *Super Mario Kart* has been ripping up racecourses in the virtual Mario Universe. And recently, the legendary speed machine was able to bust out of the screen and into real life in the mixed reality game, *Mario Kart Live: Home Circuit*. How did the tech wizards at Nintendo and Velan Studios figure out how to make a racing game that combines a virtual Mario Kart zipping around on a Switch device and an actual toy zipping around obstacles in your living room? Yosuke Tamori, Hiroki Ikuta, and Yuji Ichijo, from Nintendo, and Karthik Bala, from Velan Studios, explain.

### LET YOUR IMAGINATION GO WILD

**Karthik Bala:** Velan starts by building an awesome core team and working on ideas. We quickly start building prototypes to test different ideas until we discover something unique and fun. Once we find the fun, then we build on top of it and enhance it.

**Yosuke Tamori:** At Nintendo, we had a hardware team that created the actual kart, a software team that made the game feel like a classic *Mario Kart* experience, and a team that programmed the kart so it could be controlled by the Nintendo Switch system.

**Yuji Ichijo:** It took three years to create, which may seem like a long time, but it was fun to be able to do new things every day, and the time passed quickly.

### TEST, TEST, AND TEST SOME MORE

**Hiroki Ikuta:** Since homes around the world have many differences, like floor type and size, we first had to research different environments to race in. We found out that if you slowed the kart down to a speed that a beginner could manage, the kart could get stuck on the carpet. So, we changed the kart hardware to increase the torque.

### SOMETIMES YOU GOTTA SUPERSIZE IT

**Yuji Ichijo:** For real karts and in the classic *Mario Kart* series, the size of the driver or character is large compared to the kart. But we learned that if we used this balance for the physical kart for this game, then Mario and Luigi would've been too big and caused the kart to run less smoothly. So, we adjusted their size and the position of the camera to ensure it drives better.

### HOW TO GET INTO THE GAMING BIZ

**Yosuke Tamori:** There are always commonalities between what you like to do and want to do, and the skills needed for the job you want. For example, I enjoyed drawing, so I studied art and got a job as a video game designer.

**Karthik Bala:** You can't go wrong in learning science, engineering, and math! All of those are important aspects in developing video games. If you love to draw (and I loved to draw cars when I was a kid), there are lots of 2D and 3D art classes you can take in school/college. Above all, just stay curious about the world around you and learn how things work! The best game designers in the world are very curious people who are constantly learning new things.

## MARIO'S BEHIND-THE-SCENES PROS

**The team who created _Mario Kart Live_ included people with all kinds of training.**

- Hardware engineers created the karts.
- Programmers developed the kart's controls.
- Designers created the visuals for the game.
- Sound engineers created in-game sounds and music.
- Translators kept Japanese and U.S. teams connected.

Standard Horn

Back

A OK

## HALL OF FAME

### HERE ARE SOME OF GAMING'S OTHER GREATEST RIDES.

→ Paraglider, _The Legend of Zelda: Breath of the Wild_

→ Stagecoach, _Red Dead Redemption_

→ Koopa Clown Car, _Super Mario series_

→ Octane, _Rocket League_

→ Ferrari Testarossa Spider, _Outrun_

→ BMW M3 GTR GT (E46), _Need for Speed: Most Wanted_

→ G-6155 Interceptor, _Spy Hunter_

→ Ebon Hawk, _Star Wars: Knights of the Old Republic_

→ M12 Warthog, _Halo_

# GUY FIERI: FOOD, FAST CARS, AND FUN!

**Superchef Guy Fieri** entertains us with shows like *Diners, Drive-Ins and Dives* and *Guy's Grocery Games* and makes us drool with recipes like Mac Daddy Mac n' Cheese and Guy-talian Nachos. And even cooler than all of that, the famous TV star is also an incredibly generous person who has raised millions of dollars to help those in need!

When he's not in front of a camera or behind a stove or out doing charity work, there's one place you can likely find him: behind the wheel of one of the cars in his amazing collection. Fieri, also known as The Mayor of Flavortown, told us about his love of all things fast.

**What do you love more, cars or cheeseburgers?**
Well, if I was choosing between cars and food, it would be food. But if the question is cars or cheeseburgers? Cars. I couldn't sell out all of my cars for a cheeseburger!

**When you were a kid, were you always obsessed with cars and food?**
Obsessed is an understatement! I've always loved them both. I had the die-cast toy cars of the ones that I wanted to buy — I would just look at them and dream. I'm a big Chevy fan, and so I had Corvettes, Chevelles, C-10 pickups. And now I own them for real!

**What's that like to have your dream cars in your garage?**
We all have to find the things in our life that fuel us. You've got to set goals and start making progress. I didn't buy all of those cars at once. The first was a 1971 Chevelle — Super Sport, big-block engine — an awesome car that I still have to this day.

**Do you have a favorite motorsport?**
I love cars. I love the way cars are made, I love the way cars handle — you name it, I love it. That goes for racing. NASCAR is just unbelievable to me, the machines and the skill and fearlessness of the drivers, but I'll watch any kind of racing. I'll watch slot cars.

**Did you have a favorite subject in school?**
Lunch! I loved auto shop, wood shop, and I took home ec. I can work a sewing machine! There are times in every person's life where you need to know how to sew a button back on a shirt.

**When did you realize that you could be a huge TV star?**
That was never something I thought was going to happen. I thought I'd run restaurants and ride dirt bikes, and I would have been very happy. Being on TV? That was like saying I wanted to be an astronaut! But I just gave it a shot, and it turned into something I would never have imagined.

**Final question: Are there any speed limits in Flavortown?**
Yes. You either gotta cook it "hot and fast" or "slow and low."

## HOW DOES SPEED AFFECT FOOD?

High heat for a short amount of time gives food a crusty sear on the outside while it stays juicy on the inside (think of a steak). Low heat for a long time gets super-tender results that melt in your mouth (like Guy's famous Righteous Ribs.) Is it lunchtime yet?

# CHECK OUT GUY'S SUPERSIZED GARAGE

Inventing your own cartoon characters is super-fun. Speech bubbles are a great way to reveal your character's attitude ("Time to go fast!"), and there are little things you can do with your drawing that help show its emotions. Take a look at these examples and try working them into your own creations!

### SHY GUY

Got a quiet, nervous character in mind? Make their eyes look up and inward and the hood bowed down (like a puppy dog who is afraid they're in trouble). Also try having the wheels go in slightly different directions, like someone whose legs are nervously shaking.

### MAD DOG

Want to invent a villian (or a car that's just in a bad mood)? Draw crinkled-down eyebrows, like a hungry animal searching for prey. Add big, sharp teeth and rugged tires leaning out like they just ran over something. Get outta the way!

### SPEED DEMON

If your character loves to drive fast, here's how to make them look super speedy and excited. Give them a big grill smile, make their eyes wide open (like someone excited to open a present), and give them big ol' tires that are ready to rip!

## ? DID YOU KNOW?

BEFORE ANIMATION STARTS ON ANY MOVIE, ARTISTS CREATE STORYBOARDS, WHICH ARE KIND OF LIKE COMIC STRIPS, TO SKETCH OUT ALL OF THE ACTION. IN PLANNING *CARS 2*, THERE WERE 80,000 STORYBOARDS DRAWN! OUR HAND HURTS JUST THINKING ABOUT IT!

# FILL IN THE BLANKS
## WACKY SPY MISSION

**TOP SECRET**

Ask a friend for a word for each blank, but don't tell them what the story is about! Then read it back and get ready to laugh.

Dear Agent _____ ,
<br>YOUR NAME

We are glad that you found this note hidden inside your _____ . It was hard to
<br>NOUN

find, but since you got straight _____ 's on your Secret Agent report card, we knew you
<br>PICK A LETTER A-F

wouldn't accidentally _____ it!
<br>VERB

Your new mission: _____ has been captured by the bad guys, and we need
<br>FRIEND'S NAME

you to carry out a secret rescue. Don't tell anyone, not even _____ !
<br>NAME OF PET

You are going to need some supplies: _____ marbles, a giant _____ , and
<br>BIG NUMBER          NOUN

a/n _____ _____ . (Note: we don't know why you'd need any of
<br>ADJECTIVE       TYPE OF BARNYARD ANIMAL

those things, but better safe than sorry!)

Next get into your spy car. It should be parked in _____ 's driveway.
<br>NAME OF RELATIVE

(We let them borrow it for a quick spy mission to _____ if they promised to pick up
<br>COUNTRY NAME

_____ at the grocery store on the way back.)
<br>FAVORITE SNACK

There will be a _____ disguise in the glove compartment, and a fake ID
<br>JOB AN ADULT WOULD HAVE

with your new spy name. First name: _____ , last name: _____ .
<br>THE LAST THING YOU ATE          STREET YOU LIVE ON

Just in case the bad guys see you leaving, check into a hotel and hide there for _____ years.
<br>NUMBER

We recommend doing _____ pushups every day to stay in shape, and learning how to speak
<br>NUMBER

_____ 's language. Why? You're the super spy, you tell us!
<br>MOVIE CREATURE

When it is finally time to carry out the mission — oh wait, we just found out your friend wasn't

actually captured. They were just on the couch watching _____ .
<br>FAVORITE TV SHOW

Great job once again, Agent _____ !
<br>YOUR NAME

"Anyone need help blowing out their birthday cake candles?"

# CHAPTER 6

# AT YOUR SERVICE

## HARDEST-WORKING VEHICLES

# HELP IS ON THE WAY!

What do books and fire trucks have in common? They're both red! This chapter is devoted to amazing vehicles, used to protect and rescue people. (But as you just learned, it will not save you from corny jokes!) Marvel at these amazing vehicles and be sure to take a minute to thank the people behind the steering wheels who are dedicated to keeping us all safe.

FIRE TRUCKS COME IN ALL SHAPES AND SIZES, DEPENDING ON THEIR MISSION. THIS ONE IS DESIGNED TO GET DOWN NARROW ROADS. THE LARGEST FIRE TRUCK IN THE WORLD, THE FALCON 8X8, IS DESIGNED TO FIGHT FIRES AT AIRPORTS AND WEIGHS 60 TONS!

**FIRES FEAR THIS FLAME-EATING BEAST!**

## SOME TERMS YOU'LL SEE THROUGHOUT THIS CHAPTER:

| | |
|---|---|
| **ARMORED** | A vehicle that has protective heavy-duty plates on it to withstand attacks. |
| **AUTONOMOUS** | A driverless vehicle that can be programmed to drive itself from one point to another, avoiding obstacles without human help. |
| **LITER** | A unit of measure for liquid (picture a 2-liter bottle of soda.) |
| **WINCH** | A rope, cable, or chain that winds around a horizontal rotating drum, made for pulling or lifting. |

# RESCUER GARAGE

## THESE AMAZING RIDES AREN'T ONLY CRAZY COOL LOOKING, THEY'RE ALSO SPECIALLY DESIGNED TO SAVE LIVES!

### QUICK-RESPONSE AMBULANCE

Like emergency rooms on wheels, ambulances have all of the equipment that medical professionals need to treat people on the way to hospitals fast and comfortably. Supercool innovations in today's ambulances include being virtually connected to hospitals, so doctors are totally informed and ready to help the second the patient arrives.

### BACKCOUNTRY FIRE TRUCK

This Big Dog 4x4 wildland truck is designed to get to fires in remote areas in the countryside. Its tank can hold 1,500 gallons of water, it's got a heavy-duty winch to help tow other vehicles to safety, and the truck's no-nonsense bumper lets it smash through whatever is in its way.

## LONGEST LADDER TRUCK

The E-ONE CR 137 holds the title of the tallest ladder in North America. It can reach up more than 13 stories and stretch horizontally 126 feet!

## SUPERFAST POLICE CRUISER

This might come as a surprise, but the fastest cop car in America is actually an SUV. The 2020 Ford Police Interceptor Utility is a souped-up Ford Explorer capable of reaching 150 mph!

## OFF-ROAD ROCKSTAR

Rugged trails and tight squeezes are no problem for this super-agile machine. The Ranger Crew XP 1000 EPS HVAC Edition is prepared for firefighting or rescue operations in all climates, and Polaris has a ton of different models all specially designed for almost any operation and terrain.

## SNOW MACHINE

The 2000XL Tucker-Terra Sno-Cat is a four-passenger vehicle that has tracks designed to help it climb over snow and ice without slipping. It can drive anywhere on a mountain where injuredskiers, hikers, or climbers might be stuck.

# CAR-CRAZED CELEB
## SHAQUILLE O'NEAL

**THE RETIRED NBA SUPERSTAR IS ALSO A LAW-ENFORCEMENT OFFICER!**

Shaq has always loved cars, but since retiring from the NBA in 2011 the 7-foot-1 b-ball legend is really drawn to ones with flashing lights on the roof. The big man has pursued his big passion for giving back to the community by becoming a reserve police officer in many of the cities he has lived and played in. He was officially sworn in as a reserve officer in multiple police departments in Florida, as well as in Tempe, Arizona, and Los Angeles. He was also sworn in as a deputy in St. Martin Parish, Louisiana, and Clayton County, Georgia. The sheriff in Clayton County posted on Facebook that Shaq's official cop car was a Dodge Charger Hellcat. Hope it had plenty of legroom!

# THE RACE CAR THAT WILL NEVER, EVER WIN!

Pace cars vary from season to season and race to race. In 2021, Chevy sent this Corvette to the Daytona 500.

Meet the hard-working pace car — a speedy vehicle that participates in every IndyCar, Formula 1, and NASCAR event but never gets to win. The pace car, sometimes called the safety car, has an important job to do: Keep the races fair and the drivers safe.

During a caution period of a race (a crash or debris on the track, for example), the pace car drives ahead of the leader and reaches a predetermined safe speed that all racers have to match. In NASCAR, that is usually between 45 and 55 mph. This allows the race cars to stay in racing order while the track is taken care of. Once the track is cleared, the poor little pace car has to get off the track (giving up its "first-place" position), and the racers are free to take off again. Sorry pace car, no trophy for you!

# WHAT IT'S LIKE TO DRIVE A 150-MPH LAWN MOWER
## LOOK OUT WEEDS AND GRASS, THIS BEAST IS COMING FOR YOU!

What you are looking at is Honda's Mean Mower, a riding lawn tractor with a 200-hp engine that can go 150 mph! (For comparison, a normal ride-on mower goes around 6 mph.) If that sounds kind of scary, that's because it is. "It smells fear," *Road & Track* senior editor Zach Bowman explained after his test drive on a quarter-mile stretch of desert. He got it up to 119 mph as he crossed the finish line. "It was over before I could remember to breathe," he remarked. Don't get too excited about getting your lawn care chores done in the blink of an eye, though. The Mean Machine is really just an experiment — **Honda doesn't sell riding mowers in the U.S. Darn!**

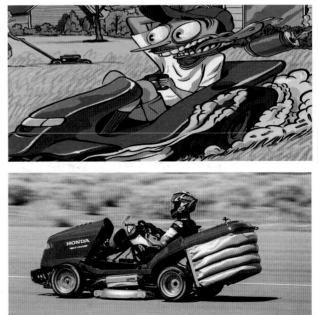

## M1A2 ABRAMS TANK

The most technologically advanced battle tank in the world, its Inter-Vehicle Information System keeps it in constant contact with friendly forces and automatically identifies and shares enemy positions. Its 1,500-hp engine gets it moving up to 42 mph. Look out!

# AMAZING ★ MILITARY

## JOINT LIGHT TACTICAL VEHICLE (JLTV)

These versatile vehicles can carry people and supplies to and from a battlefield quickly and can be fitted with armor when needed. They are big enough for tough missions and light enough to be transported where needed by helicopter.

## AUTONOMOUS VAPOR VEHICLE

Notice the driver in this odd photo? Didn't think so. That's because there is no driver! This autonomous (self-driving) vehicle was part of a robotics testing event held by the Marines, and it is spraying vapor into the air that would help hide troops and other vehicles while on the move.

## AAV-7 AMPHIBIOUS ASSAULT VEHICLE

Capable of traveling from ship to shore, the AAV-7 Amphibious Assault Vehicle is designed to deploy from Navy assault ships in the roughest seas with Marines and cargo onboard. It can transition from big waves to rocky beaches in an instant!

# VEHICLES ★

## M142 HIMARS

This 5-ton truck can carry a single six-pack of rockets or one bigger missile. HIMARS (High Mobility Artillery Rocket System) can be delivered by C-130 airplanes, allowing them to get places most heavy-duty rocket launchers can't reach.

## STRYKER COMBAT VEHICLE

It might not look like it, but the eight-wheeled Stryker combat vehicle is much lighter and easier to transport than many other tanks and armored vehicles, making it perfect for fast operations — they can hit 60 mph and travel 300 miles on one 53-gallon tank of fuel!

## COUGAR 4X4 MRAP

MRAP stands for Mine Resistant Ambush Protected vehicle. That means that this three-door, diesel-powered, 4-wheel-drive vehicle is sturdy enough to protect passengers from land mines and machine gun attacks.

# COOL JOB ALERT!

## SPECIAL AGENT DRIVER

The Transportation Section is a unit of the Secret Service whose job is to drive around and protect the president and vice president of the United States. We talked to one agent (who had to keep his name secret for security reasons) about this incredibly important job.

### What do Transportation Section Special Agents do?

We drive the presidential and vice presidential limousines, as well as certain other vehicles in motorcades. We also plan routes and work with the military to take our protective vehicles all over the world. We even wash the limousines and keep them clean!

### What type of training do agents go through?

They go through all the training regular agents go through, but they've volunteered and been selected to go to an advanced training called Protective Oriented Driving Course where they are taught race-driving techniques and are graded on their ability. It's a hard class, and only a portion of the students pass. The training is a lot of fun, because you get to drive fast, but everyone is a little nervous, because they all want to pass.

### What are some of the coolest maneuvers that you practice?

We practice for all conditions, fast and slow, and make sure we are ready to react to whatever we encounter on the road. One of the cool things we practice is called a J-Turn, where you back up really fast and spin the car and start going forward without stopping. We also practice ramming other cars, which is like bumper cars for adults.

## What type of vehicles do you use?

We start training in regular police-grade cars, then move to big SUVs, and then finally armored vehicles and the presidential limousines. The most famous limo is called The Beast, because of how big and strong it is. We train on everything we drive.

## Do you transport the same vehicles all over the world whenever the President needs a lift?

With the help of the U.S. Air Force, we fly our vehicles all over the world, but we also have multiple identical copies of all our vehicles. The president may go to several different cities across the country or the world in a single day, and whenever they step off Air Force One or Marine One, we have a presidential limousine waiting for them. The president never rides in any other vehicles while they are in office.

## If the president wants to watch a movie, are there video screens in the back? What about if they're hungry? Is there a fully-stocked mini fridge?

The president could watch a movie if they wanted to, but most of the time they aren't in the car long enough. The president has an assistant who keeps food and drinks for whenever they want them. The presidential limo does have cup holders, both for the president and the agents riding in the seats.

## Did you ever take it through a drive-thru?

The Beast is a really big vehicle, and it won't fit through most drive-thrus. If the president wants a hamburger, someone will have it waiting when they get out of the Beast at the end of the trip.

## Who gets to choose the music while you're driving?

The person you're protecting gets to choose, of course! I've heard all kinds of music.

## How did you become interested in doing this as your job?

I've always loved cars and driving, and when I got the chance to be a Secret Service Agent, I knew I wanted to drive the president. But when I was a kid, I wanted to be a fireman. I never drove a fire truck, but ended up getting to drive something way cooler.

# MIND-BLOWING FACTS ABOUT THE BEAST

★ There is actually a fleet of Beasts **ALWAYS** ready to drive.

★ One Beast costs about **$1.5 MILLION**.

★ It weighs around **20,000 POUNDS**.

★ It has **5-INCH** bulletproof glass.

★ The doors don't have keyholes — only **SECRET SERVICE AGENTS** know how to open the passenger doors.

★ If it gets a flat, it is able to drive on its **STEEL RIMS**.

★ It has a **FIRE-FIGHTING SYSTEM**, and can dispense tear gas and smoke screens.

★ When a Beast is retired, it is **COMPLETELY DESTROYED** to protect its secret components.

# HOW TO DRAW A TANK

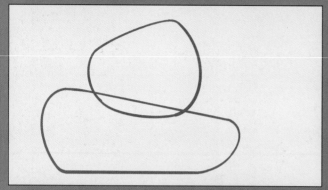

**1.** Start with two stacked shapes for the treads (bottom) and turret (top). Play with the shapes to give your tank a fun personality.

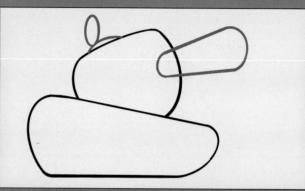

**2.** Draw a cannon extending off the turret and a driver hatch on top.

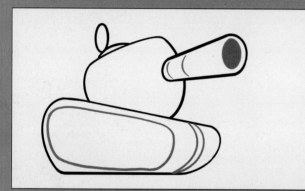

**3.** Time to add details to the cannon and give shape to the tread tracks.

**4.** Draw different-sized tread wheels and add some cool decorations.

**5.** Fill in the gap around the wheels and add lines for tread texture.

**6.** Give your tank a paint job with your favorite color and then get that cannon booming!

# ROAD DROOLS

These mouthwatering food mobiles work overtime to spread the word about their companies. **Anyone else feeling hungry?**

## RED BULL MINI COOPER

If you drive on a bumpy road, we recommend waiting at least 20 minutes before opening that can.

## OSCAR MAYER WIENERMOBILE

Gets surprisingly good mileage, 30 miles per gallon (of mustard).

## GOLDFISH MOBILE

Sorry, the cars don't come in bags of 50 like the snack.

## PLANTERS NUTMOBILE

Only take your road test in this thing if you are nuts.

## BURGER DIVE'S BURGERMOBILE

Now that's what we call a drive-thru!

## HERSHEY'S KISSMOBILE

Be sure you park it in the shade or else you are going to have a giant chocolate puddle on your driveway!

## CADBURY CREME EGG MOBILE

We won't make this egg car caption too funny — we don't want it to crack up.

123

## FORMULA ROSSA

This roller coaster at Ferrari World in Abu Dhabi is the fastest in the world — it goes 149.1 mph! Double-check that your seatbelt is fastened.

# FASTEST
# ROLLER COASTERS

### Some vehicles deliver food — these deliver screams!

## SUPERMAN: ESCAPE FROM KRYPTON

This Six Flags Magic Mountain ride features an insane 415-foot-tall tower that gets it going up to 100 mph. Hold onto your cape!

### TOP THRILL DRAGSTER

The main attraction at Cedar Point in Ohio goes 120 mph and is powered by a crazy hydraulic launcher that makes it feel like you're in a rocket!

### DID YOU KNOW?

The first roller coasters were built in Russia in the 17th century. They were giant wooden structures with frozen ramps that people slid down on ice blocks or sleds. If that doesn't sound really safe, it's because it 100 percent wasn't!

# ON EARTH

### KINGDA KA

Six Flags Great Adventure's Kingda Ka is the tallest roller coaster in the United States, and it also goes really, really fast 128 mph. Did someone say scary?

### DO-DODONPA

In a rush? Do-Dodonpa, which is found at Fuji-Q Highland in Japan, goes from 0 to 112 mph in 1.56 seconds!

"There's gotta be a rest stop somewhere near here!"

# CHAPTER 7

# FUTURE OF CARS

# THE FUTURE IS FAST!

From self-driving cars to rovers zipping around the surface of Mars, there is no limit to the amazing things that can happen when technology and imagination come together. (Speaking of limits, can you get a speeding ticket on Mars?)

## SOME TERMS YOU'LL SEE THROUGHOUT THIS CHAPTER:

| | |
|---|---|
| **NASA** | National Aeronautics and Space Administration, a part of the U.S. government devoted to air and space travel and technology. |
| **ORBIT** | The curved path of an object or spacecraft around a star, planet, or moon. |
| **PAYLOAD** | Something a vehicle is carrying that is valuable or important to its mission. |
| **PRODUCTION CAR** | Mass-produced models that are for sale to the public and comply with all of the safety regulations for road travel. |
| **PROTOTYPE** | The first model or sample of a new design or product. |

THIS IS A REAL PHOTO TAKEN FROM SPACE OF ELON MUSK'S 2008 TESLA ROADSTER WHICH WAS LAUNCHED INTO ORBIT IN 2018. THE CAR AND ITS PILOT (A DUMMY NAMED STARMAN) ARE ON A GALACTIC ROAD TRIP THAT LOOPS AROUND THE SUN AND GOES ALL THE WAY TO MARS!

THERE IS A 6 PERCENT CHANCE IT CRASHES INTO EARTH IN THE NEXT MILLION YEARS!

# CRAZIEST CONCEPT CARS

## A LOOK BACK — AND FORWARD — AT SOME OF THE MOST MIND-BLOWING DESIGNS ON WHEELS.

## HOW DOES THAT WORK?

## CONCEPT CARS

A concept car is a prototype that is made to display a carmaker's most eye-popping ideas for styling and performance. They are not built as something that will be sold soon (plus, they usually cost millions of dollars to make just one!), but are made to offer a glimpse into the future of what could be rolling — or hovering — down the road one day.

### FORD GYRON
This two-wheeled wonder from 1961 looks like it landed straight from outer space. Ford never made it into a production car, but some toy companies made mini-versions that raced off store shelves.

### CHRYSLER ATLANTIC
Long and mean, this 1995 design was Chrysler's answer to the super sleek look of a Bugatti. While people drooled over its style, it was too expensive to mass-produce, so Chrysler never made more.

### GM X STILETTO
The point of this super-pointy 1964 car? Make it look like a rocket ship. Mission accomplished!

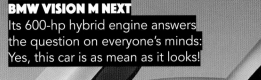

## BMW VISION M NEXT

Its 600-hp hybrid engine answers the question on everyone's minds: Yes, this car is as mean as it looks!

## MAZDA FURAI

Those flowing lines are meant to mimic the movement of water. This 2007 vehicle could have used some actual water when it was shipped to the TV show *Top Gear* — it caught fire and burned to ashes!

## DODGE DEORA

The claim to fame for this 1967 oddity? It was among the real-life cars that Hot Wheels used as models for its first batch of die-casts.

## KARMA SC2

With an all-electric motor, two seats, and the most intense scissor doors ever, this coupe sports 1,100 hp and can go 0 to 60 mph in 1.9 seconds.

## TESLA CYBERTRUCK

Elon Musk's concept truck was revealed in 2019, but looks like it rolled straight out of a 1980s video game. More than just interesting to look at, it is fast and powerful, able to tow a claimed 14,000 pounds! If production models aren't on the street yet, they soon will be.

## EZ-GO CONCEPT

A driverless, steering wheel-less vehicle designed for public transport, the EZ-GO puts safety first: It has limited speed, illuminated scrolling displays, and exterior sounds to make sure pedestrians see and hear it coming.

## GFG STYLE KANGAROO

The makers of this all-electric supercar wanted it to sit high enough so that it can deal with off-road terrain. Also? They wanted to make sure people driving behind it know which direction it's turning. Check out the size of those blinkers!

## MERCEDES-BENZ AG VISION AVTR

Inspired by the movie *Avatar*, this car of the future can move sideways, it has solar panels on its rear roof and an amazing sensor that recognizes a driver by their breathing!

## GAC MOCA

Moca is short for modular car. That means it was designed so that almost every part of its interior can be purchased and easily swapped out by its owner.

## TOYOTA CONCEPT-I

Built in 2017, it has self-driving capabilities and "Yui," an artificial intelligence agent that learns the driver's preferences and adjusts the ride to fit their mood!

# TOYOTA IS HEADING TO THE MOON

**CITROËN 19_19 CONCEPT**
All electric and all eye-popping, its engine gets it going 125 mph and, inside, each passenger basically gets their own lounge chair. The future is comfy!

**VISION MERCEDES-MAYBACH 6**
Twenty feet long, it looks like a speed boat and performs like one: Its four electric motors combine to make a total of 750 hp. You won't keep a hat on your head for long in this ride.

Toyota is going really, really, really off-road. The car company and the Japan Aerospace Exploration Agency (JAXA) announced they are working together on a new vehicle called the Lunar Cruiser, which they plan to use to zoom around the surface of the moon in 2029. The Lunar Cruiser will be the first-ever enclosed land vehicle to drive around up there and will be powered by fuel-cell electric-vehicle technologies. Besides being insanely fun to drive, it will help astronauts explore the moon's polar regions to see if visiting humans can use lunar resources, like ice. Which brings up an important question: Can you get brain freeze in low gravity?

**ROLLS-ROYCE 103EX**
Rolls-Royce had a pretty laid-back idea of the future when it made this in 2016: It doesn't have a steering wheel, or even a driver's seat. The only place to sit is on a giant couch!

# COOL JOB ALERT!

# MARS ROVER DRIVER

**MARS IS ICY, COLD, COVERED IN RED DUST, DIRT, AND ROCKS AND IS ABOUT 140 MILLION MILES AWAY. WHILE THAT MIGHT NOT SOUND LIKE THE NICEST PLACE TO VISIT, THE SCIENTISTS AT NASA FEEL DIFFERENTLY AND HAVE BEEN EXPLORING ITS SURFACE WITH ROBOTIC VEHICLES, CALLED ROVERS, SINCE 1997.**

 Dr. Vandi Verma, the chief engineer of robotic operations for NASA's Perseverance rover, explains everything you want to know about the most remote control cars in the galaxy.

### How long have you been involved with Mars exploration?
I first got involved with Mars exploration when I was at university 20-plus years ago.

### How long does it take them to get to Mars?
It takes about seven months to get to Mars. There is a launch opportunity every two years when Earth and Mars's orbits are best aligned and closest to each other.

### Do rovers drive themselves or are they remote-controlled?
Depending on the relative distance between Earth and Mars it takes between four and 22 minutes each way for a signal to travel between the two planets. So we can't remote-control the rover. Rover drivers on Earth send the rover drive commands, the rover executes them on Mars, and sends the results back. Sometimes we may provide

detailed instructions such as "steer to a heading of 30 degrees and drive 10 meters," or they can be at a high level such as "drive autonomously toward that crater and use your cameras to take images and detect any hazards such as large rocks and avoid them."

## How fast do they go?
About 4 cm/sec (a little less than 0.1 mph).

## How are they powered?
Sojourner, Spirit and Opportunity were solar-powered. Curiosity and Perseverance are powered by a radioisotope thermoelectric generator (which is a kind of nuclear battery).

## How big are rovers?
Spirit and Opportunity were 5.2 feet tall, 7.5 feet wide, and 4.9 feet high and weighed 170 kg. Curiosity and Perseverance are about 10 feet long, 9 feet wide, and 7 feet tall and weigh about a ton.

## Why put rovers on Mars?
The rovers are part of NASA's Mars Exploration Program. Their mission is to search for signs of potential life on Mars and pave the way for future human exploration.

## What has been the most surprising discovery coming from the rovers?
There was once flowing water on Mars.

## What happens if one gets stuck in a crater?
We have driven into and out of numerous craters on Mars. The rovers are designed for handling a variety of terrain. If a rover got stuck in a crater we'd try a number of strategies for getting it out. There is no roadside assistance on Mars so you can't call for help.

**MARTIAN Department of Motor Vehicles**

# CHECK OUT ALL NASA'S ROVERS AND THEIR MISSIONS

★ **SOJOURNER ROVER, 1997:** Test if rovers could land on Mars and function.

★ **SPIRIT & OPPORTUNITY ROVERS, 2004:** Look for evidence of water.

★ **CURIOSITY, 2012:** Find out if Mars's environment could support life.

★ **PERSEVERANCE, 2021:** Look for signs of ancient life and see if humans can one day live there.

AN ILLUSTRATION SHOWING HOW PERSEVERANCE DRILLS AND STORES ROCK SAMPLES IN SEALED TUBES FOR FUTURE MISSIONS TO PICK UP.

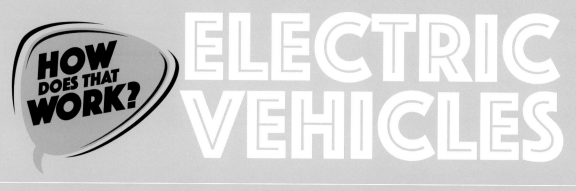

# HOW DOES THAT WORK?
# ELECTRIC VEHICLES

Take a good look at an electric vehicle (EV for short) and you'll notice something missing: a tailpipe. EVs don't need one because their motors don't use fuel, which means there are no gas or diesel fumes to release. That's great for the environment (and whoever usually has to pay for gasoline!).

A large battery pack sends power to the motor. This causes a rotor inside the motor to spin, which creates the mechanical energy that turns the gears of the car, which then rotate the wheels. Most electric cars can drive a couple of hundred miles on a single charge, and some can go even longer. Wish our phones would last that long when we get dragged to boring shopping trips!

THE ALL-ELECTRIC ASPARK OWL'S MOTOR MAKES 1984 HP AND REACHES 60 MPH IN 1.7 SECONDS!

# WILL THREE-YEAR-OLDS BE ABLE TO DRIVE THEMSELVES TO PLAY DATES?

Tesla is probably the most well-known innovator in self-driving tech, but just about every automaker you can think of is hard at work designing cars that drive themselves. Does that mean we can tear up our licenses soon? The people in government who make the rules of the road say, "Nope." As of now, the law requires that a licensed person sits behind the steering wheel of a moving car — and that all cars are built with a steering wheel in the first place!

But while we're still a long way from kids being able to cruise across town solo, you might want to know how self-driving cars actually work. Short answer: lots and lots of technology! Longer answer: A self-driving vehicle is outfitted with laser sensors, radar, and cameras. After you plug in a destination, the vehicle uses GPS and cloud computing to track its surroundings — things like traffic, weather, and road conditions. All of this data gets analyzed by an onboard computer, which tells the car to stop at that red light up ahead. (But unfortunately, it won't tell your parents that the music they're blasting is lame.)

# WHOSE FAULT IS IT IF TWO SELF-DRIVING CARS CRASH INTO EACH OTHER?

According to Thomas J. Simeone, a personal injury attorney in Washington, D.C., here's how a robo-wreck would get investigated: "Normally when there is an accident, one of the drivers is probably at fault for driving too fast, not paying attention, or following too closely. For a driverless car, the decisions about how fast to drive, when to change lanes, and how quickly to stop are made by the car's computer system and not by the driver. So, if there is an accident between two driverless cars, the companies that made the computer system for the car that was at fault will likely be liable for the accident. If a company wants to use a computer to take the place of a driver, it will be as responsible as a driver for any mistakes." Hear that, R2-D2? Keep your eyes on the road!

# A FLYING CAR

**1.** Make a slightly tilted oval.

**2.** Add a windshield (almost like you are drawing a smile) and a small square on the top for the moonroof.

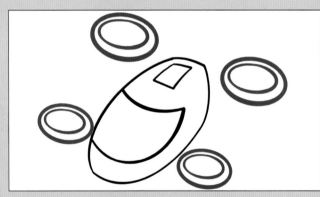

**3.** Create four donut shapes that will become its rotors and wheels.

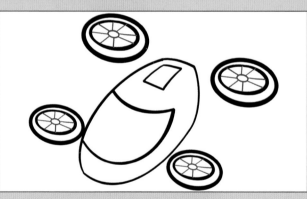

**4.** Sketch in blades to give it lift.

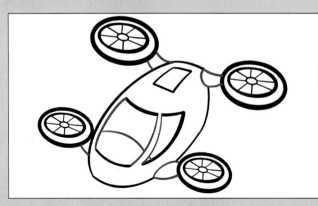

**5.** Connect the rotors to your car.

**6.** Color, add interior details, and take off!

# WHICH SPACE TRAVELER WOULD YOU BE?

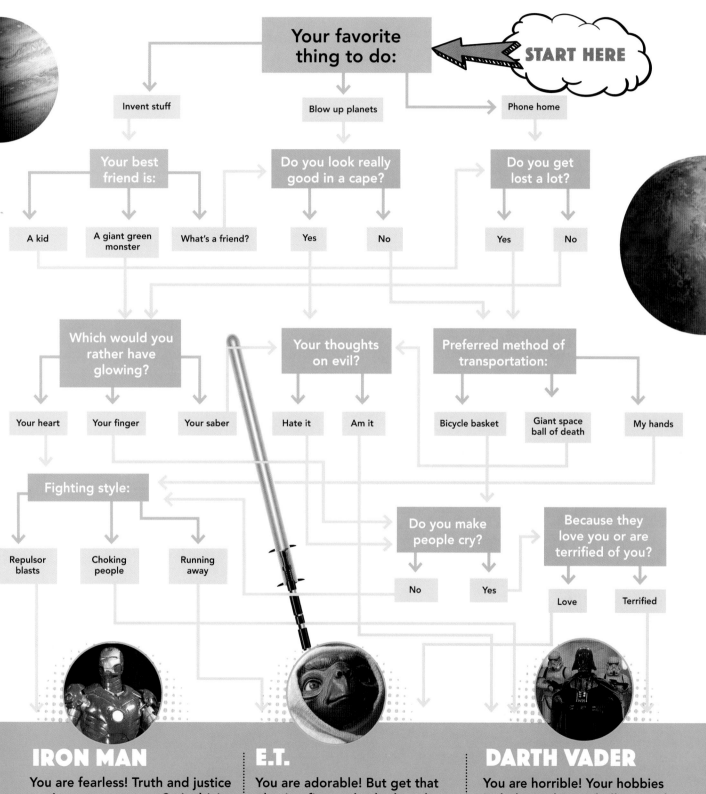

**Your favorite thing to do:**

START HERE

- Invent stuff
- Blow up planets
- Phone home

**Your best friend is:**
- A kid
- A giant green monster
- What's a friend?

**Do you look really good in a cape?**
- Yes
- No

**Do you get lost a lot?**
- Yes
- No

**Which would you rather have glowing?**
- Your heart
- Your finger
- Your saber

**Your thoughts on evil?**
- Hate it
- Am it

**Preferred method of transportation:**
- Bicycle basket
- Giant space ball of death
- My hands

**Fighting style:**
- Repulsor blasts
- Choking people
- Running away

**Do you make people cry?**
- No
- Yes

**Because they love you or are terrified of you?**
- Love
- Terrified

## IRON MAN
You are fearless! Truth and justice are important to you. So is driving around in really cool cars.

## E.T.
You are adorable! But get that glowing finger checked out by a doctor — that doesn't look right.

## DARTH VADER
You are horrible! Your hobbies include crushing rebellions and fighting with your kids. How sweet!

# ACTIVITY ANSWER KEY

**PAGE 19**
**Winner is bold.**
Corvette Stingray 194 mph vs. **Tesla Roadster claimed 250 mph**
**Denise Mueller-Korenek 183.932 mph** vs. Honda Accord 125 mph
Ferrari 812 Superfast 211 mph vs. **Lamborghini Veneno 220 mph**
School Bus 55 mph vs. **Garbage Truck 60 mph**
**Snail .029 mph** vs. Ketchup .028 mph

**PAGE 31**
Ketchup, .028 mph
Usain Bolt, 27.34 mph
Mobility scooter, 82.5 mph
2015 Porsche 918 Spyder, 214 mph
Bugatti Veyron, 253 mph
Thrust SSC, 763.035 mph

**PAGE 51**
1C, snow chains on tire
2E, dune buggy tire
3A, Mars rover wheel
4D, Amphibious military vehicle
5F, off-road tire
6B, race car tire

**PAGE 84**
A. John Cena
B. Kevin Hart
C. Lady Gaga
D. Tom Brady
E. Beyoncé
F. LeBron James
G. Manny Pacquiao
H. Kylie Jenner
I. Justin Bieber

7. 1971 Plymouth Road Runner
9. Ford Mustang GT500E
6. Light-blue Ford Bronco
5. Aston Martin DB11
8. Mercedes-Benz SLR McLaren
3. Porsche 911 Turbo S
1. Ferrari 458 Italia
2. Ferrari LaFerrari
4. Lamborghini Aventador Coupe

**PAGE 87**
Ford Flipper is the fake, the rest are really real!

**PAGE 89**
1. Chevrolet Corvette Stingray
2. Mercedes-AMG SL Roadster
3. Ford Mustang Mach 1
4. Land Rover Defender
5. Mercedes-AMG Project One
6. Lamborghini Urus
7. BMW M3
8. Ford F-150 Lightning

**PAGE 92**
1E. BMW M2 Competition
2D. Chevrolet Camaro 1LE
3A. Mercedes-AMG GT
4B. Honda Civic Type R
5C. Porsche GT3 RS

**PAGE 95**
1. White  2. Black  3. Gray/Silver  4. Blue  5. Red
6. Brown/Tan  7. Yellow/Gold  8. Green

# CREDITS

# INDEX

# INDEX

Library of Congress Cataloging-in-Publication
Data Available on request.

10 9 8 7 6 5 4 3 2 1

Published by Hearst Home Kids, an imprint of
Hearst Books/Hearst Communications, Inc.
300 W 57th Street
New York, NY 10019

Road and Track and R&T Crew are registered
trademarks of Hearst Autos, Inc.
Hearst Home Kids, the Hearst Home Kids
logo, and Hearst Books are registered trademarks of Hearst Communications, Inc.

For information about custom editions, special
sales, premium and corporate purchases:
hearst.com/magazines/hearst-books

Printed in Canada
ISBN 978-1-950785-85-8